D1615941

Mommy...Move the Sun

Beyond Dire Prognosis, Joy Shines Through

a memoir

by Jeanie Gould

ISBN-13: 978-0692316115
ISBN-10: 0692316116
Library of Congress Control Number: 2014920828

Angel Girl Publishing, Pacific Grove, CA
For information: mommymovethesun.com

*Grateful acknowledgement is made to
Vivian Greene for permission to reprint her quote.
Copyright© Vivian Greene (www.viviangreene.com)*

CONTENTS

3

Dedication 5
Author's Note 7
Introduction 9

Part One: Nikki, Birth - 3 years 13
Shattered Expectations 14
Now What? 26
Nikkiology: The Study of Nikki 36
We Are Going to Be OK 46

Part Two: Nikki, 3-5 years 59
Nikki Goes To School 60
Living Our Lives, One Day at a Time 70
Nikki's Unique Adventures 79

Part Three: Nikki, 6-11 years 85
Mommy Moments; *Some Better Than Others* 86

Part Four: Nikki, 12-14 years 101
A Lack of Options 102
Making it Happen 105
On Her Own Terms 111
Hormonal Havoc 123

Part Five: Nikki, 15-18 years 143
Her High School Years 144
That's Our Policy! 148
Celebrations with a Nikki Twist 159

Part Six: Nikki, 19 - Present 169
Nikki, All Grown Up 170
Journey to the Mariposa Home 178
Where We Are Today 183
Final Thoughts 185
Love Letters to Nikki 186
Acknowledgements 200

DEDICATION

This book is dedicated to my two special sweet peas, Brian and Nikki. You are beautiful people, inside and out. We have learned to appreciate the good times and get through the hard times without being swallowed up. I am proud to be able to say that I am your mom.

And to Steve for supporting me and making the sacrifices necessary to keep us together as a family.

I love you guys!

AUTHOR'S NOTE

Growing up on the Pacific Coast, one of my favorite pastimes was taking long walks along the beach in the sun's warm embrace looking for seashells. It was always a thrill to find that perfect shell, just sitting there in the sand, glistening in the sun. With beautiful symmetry and flawless lines, it was truly a prize to behold. Over the years, I passed over many shells with noticeable imperfections, never taking the time to check and see if they might still have something special to offer. It wasn't until my journey with Nikki that I learned the full power of this invaluable lesson.

If my world had been filled only with perfect shells, I would have missed some of life's most important lessons along the way. I might never have learned from adversity, pain, or sorrow.

Imperfect shells inspire others and demonstrate the will to go on in a way that no perfect shell ever could. They have been tested...tried...and hurt. They continue to be. They help me see the extraordinary in the ordinary.

Now when I walk along the beach gathering shells, I see that each one has its own special beauty...its own unique purpose. Thank you, Nikki.

I hope our story can help other families get through the challenges of raising a handicapped child after the dark tunnel of shattered expectations. They, too, can emerge from the experience with greater compassion, acceptance, appreciation, and most of all... hope!

(Inspired by My Beautiful Broken Shell by Carol Hamblet Adams, Harvest House Publishers, Eugene Oregon, 1998.)

INTRODUCTION

This time of year, the sun wouldn't make it to Nikki's sandbox until around noon. It was a little earlier than that today when she was raring to go. Since it was always a losing proposition to say no to her when she was in that mood, I took her out to the backyard. The dew was still sparkling on the grass from the early morning fog and Nikki ambled over to her sandbox and began to settle into her routine. She loved sitting in the sand and flicking it with her fingers. A few minutes later, after I got my gardening tools out of the shed, I noticed that she had stopped flicking and began focusing on a section of the grass.

Yes…nice grass, but what do you want with it?

Nikki just kept pointing, and I kept signing. "What?"

She stood up and came over to me, then grabbed my hand and walked me to the portion of lawn that had caught her attention. When she placed my hand directly over the only blade of sunshine in the yard, I could almost hear her saying, "Okay, so now who's the slow one?"

For Nikki, the line dividing the sun from the shade formed the perfect contrast between light and dark, warm and cold, happy and sad. Finally, I got it! My daughter was asking me to move the sun for her, to tug at the sunshine just enough to redirect those delicious rays of warmth over to her sandbox. The touching innocence of her request brought tears to my eyes. The fact that she felt I possessed the power to get her whatever she wanted and needed in life completely overwhelmed me. Of course, I would literally move the sun, the moon, and the stars for her—if I could. It made me sad that I was just human and could not fulfill her simple request. Instead, all I could do was sign to her: "Wait."

While the sun took its time moving toward Nikki's sandbox, we took refuge in that part of the yard where it had already established itself, and began bathing in its warmth. It was fifteen minutes later when the sun finally complied with Nikki's request, prompting her to toddle off and resume her sand-flicking routine. With the sun set in precisely the right position, the world was looking a whole lot brighter now.

Nikki and I have always shared a love for the sun. Our family still likes to refer to the corner between the closet and the sliding glass door in our master bedroom as "Nikki's sun nest." Whenever the sun poured through the glass door in the afternoon, Nikki would gravitate to that little space.

She would pull the pillows and blankets from our bed and make herself a comfy little nest. First, she would sit with her back to the window, luxuriating in the warmth. As she relaxed and leaned forward, a little accumulation of drool would form on the blanket in front of her. That was invariably the precursor to her lying down and falling into a deep sleep, content as a napping kitten. All balled up in front of the window, she was enjoying every last ray of sunlight.

I am now basking in the warmth of the sun coming through the window, reflecting on the ways that Nikki and I are similar. Like Nikki, I have always enjoyed the feeling of the sun on my back, as it seems to penetrate my soul and generate positive energy. Since childhood, I have loved spending summers camping at the lake…sunbathing and swimming…playing in the water…each time experiencing that euphoric tingle from the sun's warming rays.

Even though Nikki is limited by the disease that runs throughout her body, she still has a part of me in her. She is my happy, loving child and not just the disease she happened to be born with. Throughout her life, I have done my best to "move the sun" for Nikki. Sometimes I did it with the help of others, sometimes on my own. The story you are about to read reveals how Nikki has changed our lives and those of everyone else who loves her. It also tells how she has managed to move the sun for us.

✦ ✦ ✦

PART ONE
✦
NIKKI: AGE 0 - 3

SHATTERED EXPECTATIONS

As I open my memory box after so many years have passed, out comes every emotion that had been haphazardly tucked away. All the memories…the good, bad, and ugly—like a day hasn't gone by since the events took place. One piece makes me laugh out loud, another brings me to tears. The one item that stops me cold is Nikki's baby book. I had bought it at the beginning of my pregnancy with all my hopes and dreams for a perfect little child. I sigh, remembering that I had never written a single word in it. I close my eyes and the tears well up as the memories of the beginning of Nikki's life come into focus…

How did this happen? What went wrong? We are good people. Why us?

When Nikki entered this world, she was whisked away from me so fast that, even now, the memory remains a blur. I heard a voice comment that she looked as though she were on the brink of death, with the lowest possible Apgar scale. Her Catholic nurse saw the signs and administered Last Rites.

I remember waking up in my hospital room, alone. A nurse entered, and presented me with a book on the topic of grieving for the loss of a child.

"Did she die?" I asked.

"No, but it's imminent," she said.

The doctors and nurses who attended the delivery told me it would be best if I didn't see Nikki, to avoid bonding with her. I could not believe they could say that. So convinced that she wouldn't survive, they even gave me medication to dry up my milk.

Soon Steve arrived with an update on Nikki's condition. When he mentioned her long, skinny legs that resembled mine, I made my decision.

"She's our daughter, damnit, and if I want to see her, I will."

Reluctantly, the nurses took me to the intensive care nursery, where I saw our special angel for the first time.

How could a baby that sick and frail look so beautiful to me? How could a baby that small have such a daunting disease?

Nikki surprised the hospital staff, and made it through the night. Once she was out of the incubator, I spent hours in the nursery holding and rocking her. She made it through that day and then another, and then another…

Our lives had been going according to plan. We had a happy, healthy two-year-old son named Brian, and a new baby was on the way. With the help of our families, we were able to buy a small house. We both loved our jobs at the same resort and our circle of friends. Life was good and seemed to be getting better.

About seven months into the pregnancy, we made an appointment for an ultrasound, essentially to find out if we were having a girl or boy so we would know what color to paint the nursery. The procedure seemed routine until the technician set down her wand in silence and abruptly left the room. A few minutes later, which felt like an hour, she returned with a specialist. They studied the images carefully, advised me I could leave, and promptly preceded me out. As Steve and I drove home, I tried to convince myself that everything was okay. It was a hard sell.

At work the next day I got a call from my doctor, who informed me there were some concerns about our baby's condition. At that precise moment in time, the day went dark…a stark signal that our lives would never be the same again.

We scheduled the recommended appointment with a specialist and endured a tense two-and-a-half-hour drive to a prestigious hospital in San Francisco. As we walked toward the examining room, the long hallways felt dim and hostile. With every step my anxiety intensified. After the technician did an echocardiogram to check the baby's heart, I lay on the table alone for what seemed like an eternity. Then, a doctor and six medical students came in to study the images. They talked among themselves as if I were not even in the room.

Hey! Remember me? I'm still here, and this is my baby you're talking about.

I remember hearing the doctor say, "All I see here is perfect heart structure."

For a moment I clung to that shred of hope. Then he spoke again to the students. "Wait! There it is…the perfect rhabdomyoma! This child has tuberous sclerosis."

He turned to me. "I am so sorry. You can get dressed now, and your doctor will meet with you after we have consulted with him."

As soon as they left, I got dressed. Filled with dread and stunned by the insensitive treatment I had received, Steve and I went back to the waiting room.

The doctor walked in, a nonchalant look on his face. "Your fetus has a rare disease called tuberous sclerosis. It's a disease where tubers, non-malignant tumors, grow on all vital organs: the brain, heart, lungs, and kidneys. Your fetus will probably not make it to term. She's in heart failure as we speak. She has large rhabdomyomas in her heart that are obstructing blood flow throughout her body. It is pooling up in her abdomen. That alone will probably kill her before she's born, which would be a blessing due to the retardation, epilepsy, and autism that she will be faced with if she survives. All children born with this disease who survive, have to be institutionalized anyway."

We were in total shock. I felt myself sink deep into a hole. The doctor's words had taken away any remaining shred of hope.

Then he added, "It's too bad you didn't know this a couple of weeks sooner because then you could have aborted and tried to get pregnant again."

Struggling to keep my composure, I asked him what he would do if he and his wife were getting this diagnosis. He said they wouldn't bring the child into their house, as the seizures alone would be too hard to handle.

His advice was for me to disassociate myself from my child. "Pretend you're not pregnant. Drink if you want, smoke if you want, and quit taking prenatal vitamins. On the rare chance that she does survive, I would recommend you deliver her at a hospital where they aren't equipped to prolong her inevitable death." He continued by stating that our daughter's case was unique. This was the first case of tuberous sclerosis to be diagnosed in utero in the United States.

When choosing her name, we had originally settled on Stephanie Danielle. Now she wasn't going to be our child at all…she would be God's child. Her life was in His hands. That evening we searched through our baby name book again until we found the name Dominique, which means "belonging to God." As beautiful as it was, Dominique sounded a little too formal for our tastes, so we decided to call her Nikki.

When we told our boss the devastating news, he told us he knew a world-renowned specialist and suggested we see him for a second opinion. He even pulled some strings to get us an appointment. With our hopes renewed that the first diagnosis could have been wrong, we went to see the physician. But his comments were even more painful. "The most noble thing you can hope for is that your unborn child dies in utero. The sooner, the better."

What do we do now? Where do we go from here? How do I function day-to-day knowing each kick might be her last? How do we tell Brian that the baby growing in Mommy's tummy is sick?

When we got home, Brian asked us about the baby. I retreated to the bedroom in tears while Steve sat down with Brian for a talk. "The baby in Mommy's tummy is very sick. There is nothing the doctors can do. God is in charge, and whatever happens to the baby is up to Him. Talking about the baby makes Mommy very sad, so it will be better for now if you came to me to talk about it. Okay?"

Brian nodded, "Okay, Daddy." Then he toddled off to play.

It was time for some tough decisions. We talked it over with our family physician, and he agreed to deliver Nikki at our local hospital—assuming she lived that long. On the chance that she didn't, Steve made burial arrangements. Nikki was due in mid-February and since there was so much uncertainty ahead, our doctor suggested we schedule the delivery. After working around other family events, we decided on February 12th. Now, the details were set. In the meantime, we just had to try to carry on with our lives as well as we could.

During the next few months, Brian never mentioned the baby to me. A week before she was due, he asked Steve, "How's the baby now?"

Steve told him the baby was still very sick. "We don't know what God's plan is, so we will keep praying."

"Okay, Daddy," he said, before going off again to play.

When we went to the hospital on the 12th, our hearts were filled with a blend of hope and dread. With absolutely no idea how the day would end, we were secretly hoping for a miracle while at the same time trying to stay realistic. I settled in at the hospital, labor was induced, and Nikki was born.

There seemed to be little chance she would remain in this world for long. The medical staff suggested we make arrangements for Nikki to stay with a foster family, in case she survived long enough to be discharged from the hospital. We weren't sure what was the right thing to do, fearful as we were to bring Nikki home and risk having Brian see her die.

Our choice was to place Nikki in a very loving foster home nearby. I found myself visiting there all the time. Steve and I would go to see her, and then I couldn't pull myself away when it was time to leave. Although the care she received was incredible, I knew I needed her and felt she needed me.

After Nikki had been with the foster family no more than a couple of days, I told Steve, "This just isn't right. She's our daughter, and she needs to be with her family."

After he agreed, however hesitantly, we had a talk with the foster family. They were expecting our reaction, but it was still hard for them to lose Nikki—they had already built a loving bond with her. How lucky we felt to have them in our lives.

Steve and I explained Nikki's condition to Brian as best we could, knowing we could not protect him from the realities of what might happen to her. She was a member of our family for better or worse, and she was coming home.

We announced the decision to our families. Like us, they were concerned about how Nikki would change our lives. And, what about Brian? Would he be able to have a normal childhood with the baby needing so much care and attention? Some family members feared Brian's life would be ruined, and asked that we consider institutional care for Nikki.

I remembered a day early in my pregnancy when I walked past a group of disabled adults and thought I could never raise a child with disabilities. Yet here I was, having loved Nikki from the moment I saw her, and ready to take on the responsibility for her care. I knew without a doubt it was what I needed to do.

We planned a party to welcome Nikki home and to thank our family and friends for their emotional support. My heart was in my throat as our friends started to arrive in anticipation of our baby's arrival. Talk about a guest of honor! As the foster parents drove up with her, everyone in attendance turned silent. Nikki wore an angelic dress for her special day, a gift from her foster parents. She looked radiant.

"This is my baby, Nikki," Brian announced to our guests.

It was a joyful homecoming…brimming with happy tears, love, and laughter. When the party was over, it was time to settle in with our newest family member.

Brian was happy to have his baby sister home. He was a big brother now and was very proud of his new role. As Brian adjusted to sharing me, I bought him his own baby, a Cabbage Patch doll named Collin, whom he fed while I was feeding Nikki. He would wipe Collin's face, change his diaper, and put him down for his nap—the same as I did with Nikki. For a short time, our family life seemed almost normal, which we hoped would continue for Brian's sake.

Because Nikki's immune system was weak, we tried to keep her out of contact with anyone exhibiting symptoms of an illness. The doctors had prepared us to watch Nikki closely for the inevitable seizures to begin…the thought of which was terrifying.

Then, when she was one month old, Nikki began having the dreaded tongue-thrusting seizures we had been watching for. This was when Nikki's lifelong struggle with seizures and seizure medications began. Which type? What dose? What was the half life? How would it interact with the other medications she was on? There were constant trips to the hospital in order to monitor her blood levels. This was where she probably caught the virus that almost killed her. At first, it seemed like nothing more than a bad cold. But Nikki was getting progressively worse, and, at the same time, Brian came down with a double ear infection.

We were in the midst of packing for a family trip to Washington, DC for Steve's foster brother's wedding. When Steve got home from work, I gave him an update on the kids' conditions. I told him the doctor wanted to check Nikki in the morning, as her breathing had become increasingly labored and her color was getting worse. He thought he might have to admit her to the hospital. That, combined with Brian's ear infection, left us with the grim realization we would probably not be able to travel.

Steve slammed his fists on the table, and exploded. "My parents have already bought the tickets, and we're going; end of discussion."

I had never seen him this mad, and I was in shock. Words cannot express how horrible I felt. "You need to decide which family has your loyalty," I said, fuming.

We left it at that overnight, but you could have cut the tension with a knife.

At the next morning's appointment the doctor admitted Nikki to the hospital, and, considering Brian's ear infection, recommended that he not fly, as it would be too painful.

Steve was forced to decide whether or not to travel alone. Uncertain of his final decision, I arranged care for Brian, and then went to stay at the hospital with Nikki. That evening, as Nikki's condition continued to worsen and I was deep into panic mode, Steve decided to cancel his flight. We sat by Nikki's bed listening to the monitors. She was so small, so frail, and so deathly ill.

Then the phone rang. Steve answered it and went down the hall to talk. Fifteen minutes later, he returned and informed me his parents were still hoping that he and Brian would join them. Even though they had missed their original flights, they could still make it to the wedding. Speechless, I stared daggers at him. Once again, he decided to stay.

The doctor came in very late that night and, after reading Nikki's chart and checking her vital signs, he asked Steve and me to follow him into a small conference room across the hall.

"Nikki's CO2 levels are so high that her body is suffocating itself," the doctor said. He didn't think she would make it through the night.

My heart was racing, my hands were clammy, and I felt lightheaded. I was hoping to wake up soon and find out it had all been just a horrible nightmare...but that wasn't the case.

We had to decide right away if we wanted to try to extend her life, even if only temporarily, by having Medevac fly her to a large hospital in the San Francisco Bay Area where she could be put on a respirator. There would be no room in the helicopter for either of us, nor was there any guarantee she would survive the trip.

"As I see it," the doctor said, "your only other option is to keep her here with you and pray. With what I know about tuberous sclerosis, this might be a blessing in disguise. What quality of life will she have if she survives?"

He told us to talk it over and make a decision while he went to check on Nikki.

We had to decide our daughter's fate in a few minutes? It was going to take us more than a few minutes to try and process what was happening. We stared silently down at the stark table in the dreary room.

What if the doctor is right to be concerned about prolonging her life by artificial means? Does God have another plan? Should we interfere? Do we have what it takes to do this, and will we have the strength to live with the consequences of our decision?

Once we began to talk, it came down to the fact that I couldn't come to grips with not being with Nikki during transport.

I kept saying, "A baby needs her mommy."

When the doctor came back in the room, he asked us what we had decided.

I looked him straight in the eye and asked, "What would you do if this were your child?"

Unable to make eye contact, he too stared down at the stark table. When he looked up there was a tear in his eye, and he said, "I honestly don't know. What I do know is that whichever path you choose, you have to know in your hearts that it is the right decision for both you and your child, regardless of the outcome."

Steve and I had decided to keep Nikki with us, to hold her and pray throughout the night. Back in her room it was just the three of us, and it was dark and quiet except for the eerie beeps and flashes of her monitors that let us know she was still with us. The seconds seemed like minutes, and the minutes like hours. It felt like the longest night of my life.

Morning came with a hint of sparkling sunshine...and the good news that Nikki had made it through the night. We knew we weren't out of the woods yet, but we were definitely feeling more reason for optimism.

The doctor came in early, since he hadn't received the call he was expecting from the nurse. He looked at us, and then looked down at her chart, shaking his head in amazement. "Wow! Her CO_2 levels have dropped drastically! I couldn't imagine this was possible. We changed her antibiotic, but I didn't think it would be enough, soon enough. He shook his head again, and smiled. "Well, she proved me wrong...again!"

That was when the floodgates opened for me, and I couldn't stop crying. I hugged the doctor, Steve, Nikki, and any nurse I could wrap my arms around. Then my legs felt wobbly, and I had to sit down. I had used up all my strength to get through the night with some semblance of dignity. And now, nothing was left. It took me a while to recoup.

Although Nikki had turned the corner, she would have to stay in the hospital for quite a while. To us, her recovery represented a miracle. To the doctors, it remained a mystery. Call it whatever you like, the one thing everyone could agree on was that our special girl had demonstrated an incredibly strong will to live.

A few days later, while I was still in the hospital with Nikki, a nurse brought me an unopened manila envelope. She told me the doctor had received it anonymously, and that it was for me. The attached note said: "For your new patient with tuberous sclerosis." Inside, I found several brochures from the Tuberous Sclerosis Alliance which was located in Maryland. I had never seen them before, and I hadn't even known that an organization in support of the disease existed. My pulse quickened as I began to read...and the more I read, the quicker it raced. One brochure, from the Tuberous Sclerosis Alliance provided a helpline phone number.

Oh, my God. We're not alone.

I read further on, and learned about a few cases much less severe than those we had previously heard about.

I called the helpline to introduce myself and explain the situation with Nikki. The voice was friendly and comforting and it felt good to talk with someone who understood. I asked lots of questions, and although I don't remember everything she said, I do recall her saying, "Of course there is hope, honey!"

With those few simple words, she began turning the darkness back to light.

Nikki was getting better every day. By the tenth day, we got the green light to take her home. Unfortunately, this episode had compromised the health of her lungs, and it left her much more susceptible to bouts of pneumonia throughout the first three years of her life.

Within a few months, we tracked down the people who had sent us our 'hope in an envelope.' It was a beautiful local family who also had a daughter with tuberous sclerosis. We bonded with them immediately, and our friendship continues to this day.

✦ ✦ ✦

I had done everything right during my pregnancy. I was no less careful than I was during my pregnancy with Brian. I ate right, I cut out all diet sodas, I didn't drink alcohol or smoke, I exercised and was religious about taking all my prenatal vitamins. The only thing different this time around was that I didn't get as much rest as with Brian. I was working part-time at the resort, taking care of my family, and moving into a new home.

I think it is human nature for a woman to blame herself when something goes wrong with a pregnancy, since it is inside her body that the fetus grows and is nurtured. I started playing the guilt hand with myself, and I was losing. Revisiting my pregnancy journey, day by day, I was trying to isolate anything I could possibly think of that might have contributed to the challenging outcome.

Due to a slight risk to the fetus, I had chosen not to have amniocentesis. Now, second-guessing my decision, I thought maybe I should have gone ahead with it. When I mentioned this to our doctor, he assured me that Nikki's disease was so rare that there wasn't a test for it, anyway. "You could then have been faced with another tough decision," he said. "What would you have done if there had been a test, and we found out about her disease early enough before her birth to terminate your pregnancy?"

That's another road I don't want to go down.

Desperately searching for a definitive answer, I confessed to my doctor that I remembered drinking a small glass of diet soda one day, as that was all that was available at a picnic I attended. "Could that have done it?"

He reassured me, "Absolutely not."

How about the bad case of bronchitis I had about the time I got preg-

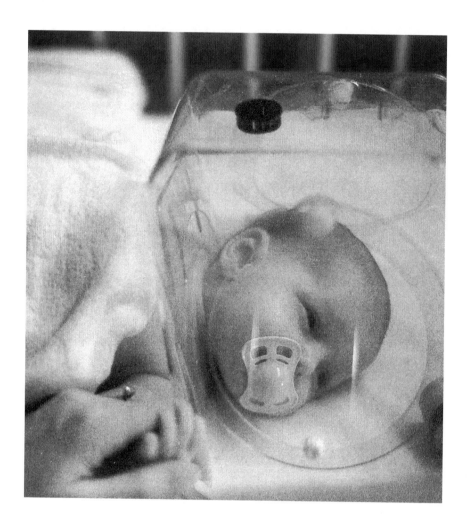

nant? Could the antibiotics I took have contributed to this?"

"Come on, Jeanie! Quit blaming yourself. You did nothing wrong. This was out of your hands."

Maybe, but will we ever know for sure?

What we knew about this disease with certainty was that it was caused by a rare mutation of a chromosome—usually, but not always, genetic. We learned the telltale sign for the disease was an ash-leaf shaped, non-pigmented area on the skin. Doctors told us they could check for these lesions on Steve and me with a Wood's lamp, to see if either of us were carriers. We opted for the tests.

Steve and his family were going through their own version of guilt hell. His dad was adopted and didn't know much about his biological family. He did recall that one of his siblings had some sort of handicap, but he knew little about it. Since they lived close by, Steve's parents decided to be tested, as well. Ultimately, all test results came back negative, generating multiple sighs of relief. The blame each of us had been claiming for our own, as it turned out, belonged to none of us.

Yes, the situation is still daunting, but we just have to accept that we're some of the chosen few.

NOW WHAT?

My emotions were out of control. I was confused, frustrated, lonely, and sad; I didn't think I would ever be able to smile again. I knew I needed help, but I didn't know which way to turn. If the doctors didn't have the answers, who did? Moral support I could get, but I found no local resources that could offer professional guidance, and the Tuberous Sclerosis Alliance had no local chapter. I tried reading books about bad things happening to good people, but none of those helped.

I had never gone to counseling before, but if I ever needed an expert shoulder to lean on, it was now. So I started asking around and was given the name of someone to try. As difficult as it was for me to start the process, I called and made an appointment…hoping for a miracle.

As soon as the counselor opened the door, I sat down and started spilling my guts to this total stranger. Beginning with the ultrasound and on through Nikki's birth and beyond, I described everything that happened in detail. His eyes opened wider and wider as I spoke and he took on a shocked expression. Then I saw tears trail down his cheeks as he proceeded to confess he was also going through a hard time, as his beloved father had just passed away. By the end of the session, he expressed how sorry he was for my family, and I left feeling bad for him. In the end, neither of us had done the other any good.

Okay. I just paid $90 for a therapist to cry over my story.

What I had wanted was for someone to reassure me that this was not the end of the world and that I had what it took to raise Nikki. That wasn't what I got. I decided not to try counseling again unless I could find a counselor who had a special-needs child; one who would understand first-hand. In one of my most desperate moments, I even wished that one of my friends was raising a special-needs child of her own, so I would have someone with whom to commiserate. I needed someone who understood what I was going through. I knew this was wrong, and I was ashamed of myself for even thinking it. My rational side would never consider such a selfish scenario, but it was my out-of-control emotional side that was currently in charge, and I was keeping those feelings to myself.

Weeks later, at Nikki's next doctor appointment, I told her pediatrician about my experience with the counselor. Since he was a good listener, and I saw him more frequently than almost anyone, I felt comfortable confiding in him. He told me about a local parents support group, and suggested I give it a try. I looked forward to attending their next meeting, but Steve was not as thrilled with the idea. He seemed to be operating in a state of denial, going to work every day pretending his life was still normal. The last thing he wanted was to go to a meeting attended exclusively by parents of children with disabilities. I convinced him we needed to try it, that we were in this together. In order to go to the evening meeting, I had to find a babysitter to stay with Brian and Nikki, which was no easy task. I needed someone in whom I had confidence, someone who felt comfortable dispensing medications, monitoring seizures, changing diapers, and on down the list. If I were to find the right person, I would also have to be in a position to pay their higher rate. Also, before leaving her in charge, I would have to measure Nikki's meds, prepare dinner, and go over the emergency contact numbers.

I had such high hopes as Steve and I arrived at the meeting. The chairs were in a circle, about half of them full. Everyone was chatting while waiting for the meeting to begin. There were couples and singles, and they all had a story to share. We sat down not knowing a soul and having no idea what to expect. I was not sure why, but I had butterflies in my stomach… as if this were an important test I was about to take, with a lot riding on the outcome.

The facilitator began by introducing herself and explaining the purpose of the group. We then went around the circle and introduced ourselves and talked about our special children. What I remember most was the huge pit that was gnawing away at my stomach. After listening to everyone's sad story, I noticed a pattern. The parents had described their children as if they were the disease or disability, and not merely their beautiful children who happened to have a disease or disability. Huge difference!

Since Steve and I were the newbies, we were the last to speak. After introducing ourselves, I told the group about Nikki and what she had been through. Then I hesitantly asked if we could go around the circle again and share something unique and endearing about each of our children. At that point, all of the heads turned toward me in disbelief, and I felt like an alien being. That familiar feeling of loneliness and isolation enveloped me again. Apparently, my idea had no takers and would not be making it to the evening's agenda. With that realization, I decided to fade into the background again and just listen. But the more I listened, the more convinced I was that this group was not for me. Once again, my hopes were dashed. I had tried two standard approaches for getting help, and neither was working.

What's wrong with me? I realize each person has their own methods of coping with challenges, but for some reason, I don't feel like the norm. In fact, I'm feeling even more isolated. What or who is there to help me now?

I was grasping at straws, but I didn't want pity. What I wanted was for someone to lay out a specific plan for me to follow, a direct course of action in an area where there may not have been one.

As the meeting was drawing to a close, the facilitator asked that we consider a metaphoric question prior to the next meeting. And even though, for me, there would not be a next meeting, what she said struck a chord that has remained with me through the years.

> *"Envision yourself as Jesus carrying the cross into this room tonight…the cross of your burdens. Then, after hearing everyone else describe their own crosses, think about whether you would be willing to trade crosses with any one of them… or would you simply prefer carrying your own"?*

I think that was the kick in the ass I needed. At this point, I knew we just had to do what we'd been doing. And keep on doing it. Each day would bring its own challenges, and we would have to meet them head-on. Yes, I was new to this challenge, and I had a long dark road ahead of me, but I knew I was up for the trip. I had no choice. My daughter's life depended on my ability to carry on…to move the sun for her.

One rainy morning, I was sitting in the pediatrician's office with three-month-old Nikki, waiting anxiously to find out if she was at the beginning stages of another bout with pneumonia. The first one had almost killed her, so naturally I was more than a little worried. There was only one other adult, a young mother, in the waiting room at the time, and she seemed very anxious. I didn't understand why, as her baby boy looked perfectly healthy to me.

She told me how scared she was that her baby was not nursing properly and that she was concerned that he wasn't getting enough nutrients.

Wow, I would feel so lucky if that was my only problem. This mother hasn't a clue how easy she has it. If she only knew!

The woman confided in me that she was probably being overly cautious about a seemingly minor issue, but she just couldn't calm down.

Oh no, can she read my mind?

Then she told her tragic story. Just in the last year, all three of the men she loved—her husband, her father, and her brother—had either died naturally or been killed in an accident. With all of them gone so suddenly, her son was all she had left. I couldn't fathom what she had been through, or understand how all of this tragedy could happen to one person in so short a period of time.

I should not have jumped to conclusions. For me to be playing the assumption card this early in the game, I must be holding a pretty big pity party inside my brain.

Trying to snap out of it, I reminded myself I wasn't the only one with a sad tale to tell. Everyone's got one, even if the wounds aren't immediately apparent. This was a good time for me to keep my own story to myself. As we were called into our respective doctors' offices, we hugged and blessed each other with sincere good wishes. I am still grateful to her for the lesson she taught me that day.

Still grasping for answers on what lies ahead for us raising a child with tuberous sclerosis (TS), we realized we would have to reach out further than our local community. I remembered how helpful the Tuberous Sclerosis Alliance had been while we were in the hospital with Nikki, so I decided to contact them directly. They told me about an upcoming conference for

TS families that would be held, for the first time, on the west coast in San Diego. After discussing it with Steve, we decided it was our best chance to learn and meet with others facing similar challenges. Our families agreed to care for the kids while we were away, so we made our flight reservations and did all of the necessary prep, trying to make it as easy as possible for our parents to take over.

On the first day of the conference, I felt like an anxious student entering an accelerated class in a complicated foreign language, and not one that I would use only short-term, like for a vacation. This was for a lifetime commitment, and I would have just two days to absorb and master the knowledge. From the outset, I had to remind myself to keep my emotions at bay so I could learn as much as possible for Nikki's sake. Multiple specialists were scheduled to speak on the many different medical and behavioral topics relating to TS. As the welcoming session was coming to a close, I looked down at the program to check out the first speaker, and I instantly froze. There was "his" name, the name of the doctor who preformed the echocardiogram. He was the one who said to the medical students, "There it is... a perfect rabdamyoma...," and to us, "Your child has tuberous sclerosis, I am so very sorry." Speechless, I turned to Steve and pointed to his name in the program. At first, Steve didn't make the connection, but when he watched my face turn pale and my body go rigid, he knew something was wrong. I pointed again, and this time he recognized the name and dropped his head.

The doctor reached the podium and faced a crowd of desperate families that were hungry for his knowledge. As they all clapped, I sat frozen. In his opening statement, the doctor cited a unique and interesting case he had recently diagnosed. He said that this particular case was the first in the United States in which a fetus was diagnosed with tuberous sclerosis while still in utero. "Oh my God... he's talking about us," I whispered to Steve.

Describing the case as a triumph for him, as a physician, he never considered the tragedy it represented for us, the affected family. On the darkened screen behind him the doctor projected images of Nikki's premature damaged heart, as hundreds of strangers looked on. None of them knew that sitting in their midst were the fetus's parents, with even more severely broken hearts than the one they saw on the screen. As the doctor droned on, his words merely echoed in my brain. After finishing his presentation, he asked for questions. Someone in the audience asked if the patient in the slides had survived. His emotionless answer still haunts me: "She was in heart failure at the time, so I highly doubt it."

Now, I had a new mission. As soon as the doctor finished speaking, I tried to stand up, but Steve blocked me and asked, "Where are you going?"

I told him I was going to set the doctor straight. His only response was, "Please don't pull his lungs out through his throat."

"I have no intention of doing anything like that... I only plan to 'maim' him a little."

After Steve grinned and released his grip, I marched up on stage, got the doctor's attention, and blurted it out. "I think you should know that the case you just discussed with the help of those slides was that of my amazing daughter and, against all odds, she's still with us."

Taken off guard, all he could say was, "Oh? Okay."

My mind was reeling.

That's it? That's all you have to say? How callous can you be?

With that painful punch in the gut, I ran up the stairs to find the closest restroom where I could let loose of my erupting tears. Sitting behind a closed stall, I tried to compose myself and breathe deeply. Then I heard other mothers enter the restroom and begin conversations that I wasn't sure I wanted to hear. But how could I resist? I needed to learn. The women were comparing notes about their teenage daughters with TS that were totally disrupting their lives... pulling TVs off the wall, knocking down total strangers on the street, and causing pure havoc in their lives. But Nikki was so small and sweet, I couldn't imagine her doing anything like that. It was hard enough to deal with the present, let alone think about what might happen in the future. The entire line of dialogue became too overwhelming. I had to compose myself long enough to get out of there. I was determined not to hear any more.

So much for taking the emotional side out of this.

All the rest of the presentations were easier to listen to, and we were able to muddle through. After the conference was over, I bought a book that had been recommended to me on TS, which I opened to read once we were settled in our seats on the plane. There were photos of patients of all ages inflicted with TS, each with a caption describing the physical maladies they faced. I started getting that same pain in my gut as I had in the restroom when confronted with moms sharing their heart-wrenching stories.

Deep breath, Jeanie. Take a slow, deep breath, and exhale. Repeat...

After we returned home, I made an appointment to talk with Nikki's pediatrician about what had happened at the conference, and how it made me feel. His immediate reaction was, "Burn the book! Don't project things that might not happen. We are each individuals with different make-ups and will respond differently to all situations. None of us knows what's in store for us in the future. Just take one step at a time, one day at a time."

I went home that evening, built a fire, and with a silent prayer, I threw in the book and watched it go up in flames. A calming sense of relief came over me.

✦ ✦ ✦

Still at home with Nikki, unable to go to work or socialize, I was feeling extremely isolated. It felt as though everyone else was going on with their lives as before, except me. While I knew that wasn't the case, I also knew that I was the only one living hands-on with Nikki's disease, day in and day out, twenty-four hours a day. I was certain no one understood what I was going through emotionally. On the outside, I just kept putting one foot in front of the other, but on the inside, I was still crying out for help.

That is when Nikki's doctor recommened that I reach out to our local regional center, an agency designed to help those with disabilities. I did just that, and when I found out we qualified, I felt a glimmer of hope. I was introduced to our regional center caseworker and I preceded to tell her how I was feeling, and didn't know where to turn. She mentioned that our county had an Infant Stimulation Program for Nikki, and thought that it would be a great place for me as well, to meet other people in similar circumstances.

As it turned out, this was far more than just a program for three-month-old Nikki. It gave me ideas about working with her at home to stimulate her development, and, equally important, it provided me with a much-needed support group. I found myself looking forward to our weekly gatherings. And, as amazing as it seems after all these years, one of the participating infants at that time, Danielle, is Nikki's roommate today. The two of them have been best friends all this time, which has been a blessing in itself.

We participated in the program for almost three years, in between Nikki's illnesses and hospital stays. During that period, the instructors gave us some practical ideas about how to advocate for our children in the future. Even though I learned alot I still found out the hard way that there was a lot more to learn. We were in a cycle of hospital stays, followed by time at home recuperating. The days seemed to get longer and longer, as they collided into each other without a break. Eventually, I learned from our caseworker that as Nikki's caregiver, I qualified for a few hours of respite care per week, and that she could authorize it for me. The thought of a break was very appealing, but I wondered if anyone else would be able to care for Nikki the right way. Would they notice the subtle nuances of her seizure activity? Could they give her meds without her spitting them out? And, most important, would they be gentle and caring with her? I was assured that their home care agency would only send qualified, thoroughly screened, and trained personnel with strong medical backgrounds. To seal the deal, the caseworker warned me that if I didn't take care of myself, I wouldn't be able to take care of my family. I decided to heed her warning.

Knowing that everything with an agency takes a long time, I was anxious to start the process. I decided to get one of those new cell phones, so I could be reached at any time in case of an emergency. At that time, the devices were the size of a small loaf of bread. They were also expensive and uncommon. I knew I was ahead of my time, carrying around a now-trendy hobo-style purse for the sheer purpose of transporting a phone.

In time, everything fell into place, although, while I was going through the process, it felt like waiting for all the stars in the universe to align. The respite worker would be arriving at eleven that morning and I sat with Nikki in my arms, asking her what I should do with my two-hour break. It had been so long since I'd had time for myself, and I truly had no idea what to do with it. How sad was that? Did I have a hobby? No. How could I? I had two kids, one of whom was very sick. Should I go shopping? With what money? I finally decided to use my respite to go to the library and look for something to read to the kids after Brian got home from pre-school. If I had time, I would also go for a walk on the beach.

The respite worker came and we made our introductions. I proceeded to explain all of Nikki's needs in detail, and I left her with an emergency plan as long as my arm. She politely told me not to worry, that everything would be fine. Apprehensively, I left and drove to the library. I hadn't been there in years. I even had to ask where to find the children's section. Once I entered the designated room, I sat down on the floor to begin scanning the book titles on the lower shelf. A strange noise from the other side of the room broke my concentration. It sounded like someone trying to clear their throat. After the first time, I didn't look up because I thought it seemed rude. After the second time, I wondered what was up with that? Three times in a row, and I had to check it out. I was soon sorry I did. There, in the corner of the room, was a man sitting cross-legged with his pants down around his ankles, and pointing to his very lively private parts!

Holy crap! A flasher is loose in the library—in the children's section, no less! Get me out of here!

I stood up so quickly, I got lightheaded. My wobbly legs managed to get me out of the room and to the front desk. I began stuttering to the clerk. "I...I...I just saw...did you see him...?"

All I got was a blank stare.

I was breathless. "The man...he...he...he ran out of that door over there...the side door..."

"I'm sorry, ma'am. I don't..."

They had just missed the whole thing. Shaken, I went directly home and canceled all of my newly scheduled respite visits. It took me a while before I got up enough nerve to try again, but I never returned to that library.

The walls were closing in on me, and I felt almost at the end of my rope, holding on to the few threads that had yet to be frayed by my life's ongoing challenges.

Would they be enough to hold me? I need to know.

It was a cold, gray Saturday. I could almost see the invisible bars on the windows prohibiting us from leaving the house. Nikki had a terrible case of diarrhea. Having already figured out that wearing a filled diaper was not a comfortable state of being, she would continually try to empty the contents and share it with the world. At the time, our world had narrowed to the tight confines of our living room and bathroom, and keeping it clean and tidy was a major challenge. At the same time, I was trying to keep Brian entertained. We had built a fire and were playing a board game on the living room floor. Nikki's stomach kept gurgling and the resulting eruptions kept interrupting our play time.

How many more times will I have to clean up her mess today? How can she manage to touch everything so quickly, spreading her wealth as she goes? And how much longer can I keep going? Keep your game face on, Jeanie. You have to be strong for Brian.

The interruptions had been going on for hours. Brian had gotten used to them, and would just quietly wander off to his bedroom to play with his Ninja Turtles.

I had reached my melting point and collapsed onto the bathroom floor, where I started to cry. As I tried to catch my breath, I pleaded in a desperate voice, "What am I going to have to do, get her a straitjacket?"

Responding to my outcry, Brian walked into the bathroom and asked, "Mommy, what's a straitjacket?"

Ouch! Not good. He had caught his mommy in a desperate place. As a parent, I knew how important it was that my kids looked to me to care for them in any situation, no matter what. From my sitting position on the floor, I fumbled for an answer. "A straitjacket…that's a…a kind of coat with…uh, sleeves…to keep Nikki's hands from getting into her diaper…"

"But, Mommy, then she couldn't hug us. Could she?"

That was it! The self-inflicted dagger had been introduced, and my guilt took control of the twisting. In my crumpled state, I convinced myself that the dagger must have punctured a lung, which accounted for the loss of oxygen I was experiencing. I felt like a lifeless, wilted balloon, flattened to the floor.

Deep breath! Get it together, Jeanie! Realizing that my three-year-old son had just showed me how to keep going, I sat up and inhaled.

NIKKIOLOGY: THE STUDY OF NIKKI

By the time Nikki was eighteen months old, she needed medication for increased seizure control and was referred to a neurologist. We drove over two hours to San Francisco and then waited an hour for our appointment. The doctor listened to our description of Nikki's condition. Without even changing the expression on his face, he wrote out a prescription for a new medication and told us to come back in two weeks.

That's it? That's why we drove all the way up here?

"Wait," I said. "I have questions. This is a mind-altering drug. What are the side effects? Will it interact with her other medications? How quickly should we see results? Are there other options if this doesn't work?"

He looked me in the eye and spoke sternly. "I'm the doctor and I will tell you what medications to give your daughter. You're the mom, and your job is to change her diapers."

It was quickly made clear to me that this was not to be a match made in heaven, not even close. But that didn't stop me from finishing my list of questions. "I'm also concerned that Nikki doesn't react to loud noises like the vacuum cleaner, nor does she respond when I call her name. Should we have her hearing checked?"

The doctor's immediate response was, "Deafness is not part of this disease. You just have to come to grips with the fact that your child is retarded!"

Steve and I looked at each other, and we could read each other's minds. We got up, took the prescription, and left without another word. When we got home, I went straight to our pharmacist. I showed him the prescription and asked if I could see a copy of the drug's multi-folded, microprint, user-unfriendly side-effect sheet. The pharmacist pointed to the section of the sheet that indicated the drug was not recommended for children under two to three years of age. He explained the reasons, and suggested I check with Nikki's pediatrician for another option.

From our experiences thus far, I was learning that you have to follow your gut...to put mother's intuition into action. No one out there had the specific answers I so desperately wanted. Every doctor had their own opinion which, in these complicated cases, tended to vary. You learn fast to never take anything at face value. You have to get engaged, research your options, and learn as much as you can about each specific issue you face.

Our pediatrician had been our primary doctor since Nikki's birth and we trusted him implicitly. After consulting with him, we threw away the prescription from the San Francisco neurologist, and, with his help, we began the search for another specialist. Eventually we found another one over two hours from home. She worked with us successfully for over a year, before she was transferred to a hospital back East.

After discussing my concern about Nikki's hearing with our pediatrician, he referred her to a prestigious audiology clinic for testing. This meant driving over 200 miles to the clinic for weekly tests. After two months without consistent results, an Auditory Brainstem Response (ABR) test finally verified nerve damage. Nikki was deaf. Our little angel would now be classified as having multiple disabilities.

Based on her medical history, they were able to conclude that Nikki's deafness was due to one of two probable causes: either the lack of circulatory oxygen to her tissues while she was in heart failure in utero or the antibiotic that saved her life the night she was so sick. This ototxic drug is known to cause nerve damage when blood levels become too elevated. We will never know if it was one or the other, or neither. But, at this point, did it really matter?

Steve's mom, Donna, had met me at the audiology clinic for the appointment when we were given the final diagnosis on Nikki's deafness. We were both stunned when we walked out, and we didn't know what to do next.

We spoke in unison. "What now?"

Donna's solution was retail therapy at the shopping center across the street. Mine was a Margarita. We agreed to both. Nikki scored a cute pair of pink leather shoes before each of us headed on home.

As I was driving, I kept reminding myself, this is just another speed bump. There are options out there: hearing aids, sign language. No problem. It wasn't until I'd been driving for almost an hour that I realized I was heading north, instead of south—the opposite direction of home. How could I have been so unaware of my surroundings, not noticing the road signs along the way? I had to admit I wasn't as calm as I had convinced myself I was. This was not just another speed bump. This was another lifelong hurdle. It turned out to be a long drive home.

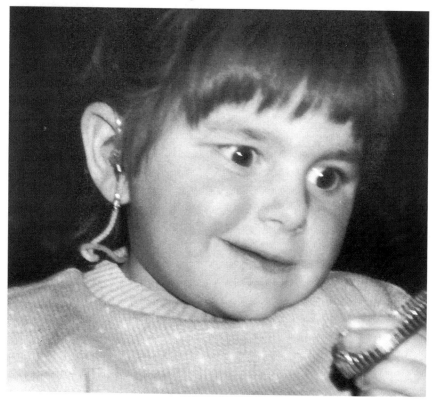

With this most recent diagnosis, we now had to add an audiologist to our growing list of medical specialists. Would Nikki benefit from hearing aids? Would her slower rate of processing defeat the benefits attained? What type of equipment would she need, and, more practically, how were we going to afford it? We would never know unless we tried, we figured, so we would give the hearing aids our best shot.

We soon discovered this would not be an easy task. There were endless trips to test different hearing aid settings, and to get proper fittings for ear molds. As Nikki grew, the molds had to be resized repeatedly. We had to test the batteries every day before putting on the hearing aids. Then, Nikki would inevitably pull them out, and we would have to start all over again. Out of necessity, we came up with an idea to add a strap between them, which we pinned to her shirt. Despite our conscientiousness, about every six months we would have to replace those expensive devices, as she was determined to yank them out of her ears. She either effectively managed to lose them, or she simply threw them into the toilet, bathtub, or anywhere other than where they belonged. Once in a while, it seemed as though she forgot she was wearing them. But then, whenever she laid down, the hearing aids would begin to squeal in her ears, and out they came again. It was a constant struggle to keep her from dislodging them.

We began endless sessions of speech therapy twice a week to help Nikki recognize, and make some sense of, whatever sounds she was hearing. I held onto the hope that someday she would be able to verbalize them in some way. Through it all, I was praying for the moment I would hear her call me Mommy. Steve and I would get excited whenever we saw progress and frustrated when she seemed to slip backwards. We rode this roller coaster for two years, hoping for that magic moment when it would all click. It never happened. The therapist concluded that the combination of her seizures, the dulling effects of her seizure medications, and her slower processing rate worked together to sabotage our efforts.

We still kept her wearing the hearing aids, hoping that total communication—some verbal with sign language—could be an option. We were basing our decision on our belief that some sounds would be more beneficial to her than silence. After about two years or so, it got to the point where even the slightest possible benefits she might have been getting from them were far outweighed by the endless battle to get her to keep them in place. Finally, with the consensus of Nikki's doctors and her speech therapists, it was decided to simply eliminate them and accept that this was part of our new reality. We then found ourselves at the beginning of another steep learning curve. Nikki would be communicating solely through sign language as best she could, and we were immersed in learning a new language.

Early on, we learned that we could either build our entire lives around Nikki's needs or we could work hard at building them into our existing daily framework. Our goal was to make our lives fit into both worlds, neither one trumping the other. This was easier said than done in some situations. This became evident when Nikki was around two-and-a-half and we decided to take our first family trip. We never dreamed that Nikki's disease would throw us into such a tailspin.

✦ ✦ ✦

One of my favorite family traditions, started by my parents, was our annual pheasant hunt in a small farm town in eastern Oregon. Every year, in early October, all my family would come together to camp for a week on a friend's ranch and hunt those illustrious birds. I have always thought it was more about the families getting together and the love and laughter that was generated rather than the actual hunt. But I am not so sure everyone in the family would agree with me. Throughout my childhood, I never missed one of these family get-togethers, and I was determined that Nikki wasn't going to, either. I wanted all my family members to bond with her and treat her just as they would any other grandchild, niece, or cousin.

We had been camping for three days and everything was going even better than I had expected. My major concern was that Nikki had never slept through the night, and a lot of us were staying in one motor home. So far, she had risen to the occasion and I was very proud of her. On the fourth day, however, Nikki's skin started to feel a little warm to the touch, and we discovered that she was running a low-grade fever. Thinking it was probably just a cold brought on by the significant change in climate, we gave her some baby aspirin and kept a close eye on her—hoping that she would be herself by morning.

When everyone got up early to get ready for the hunt, I was feeling a little left out. I had always been a part of the hunting group and I loved spending time with the guys. This year, a new tradition began. I would stay at camp with Nikki and my mom.

Nikki's fever stayed pretty low all morning, but as the day progressed, it gradually got higher. Since I knew that fevers could cause seizures, I was getting concerned, despite the fact we hadn't missed a single dose of her medications.

Just as the guys came back from their afternoon hunt, Nikki had a hard seizure. Her fever spiked and one seizure ran into the next until she went into full-blown status epilepticus. We felt so helpless watching our small, precious daughter enduring this hard, constant string of seizures. With the closest hospital about thirty minutes away, Steve and I left Brian with my parents and we jumped into the Jeep with Nikki. While Steve drove like a bat out of hell to the hospital, I held Nikki tight while she was convulsing. Out of nowhere, two pheasants flew right into our line of vision. One of them hit and shattered the headlight and the other cracked the windshield. In our desperation, we just kept going. After what seemed like an eternity, we saw a blue "H" sign and knew we were close to the hospital.

The place looked more like a small medical clinic than a hospital. Nikki was taken immediately into the emergency room. No one there had heard of tuberous sclerosis or seen anyone in status epilepticus. The doctor realized that what he was seeing was beyond his ability to treat. At a loss for what to do, he asked me to call Nikki's pediatrician for assistance. I was so shaken that I had trouble remembering the number, despite the fact it was deeply embedded in my brain. I finally managed to reach his office, only to learn that Nikki's doctor wasn't in. At that desperate point, it was arranged for Nikki to be transported by Medevac life flight helicopter to the nearest large hospital. When the helicopter arrived, the emergency personnel whisked Nikki on board. I ran out with them, ready to get in with her, but was told it wasn't possible. There was just enough room for Nikki and the specialized nurse.

"You can't be serious," I said. "She's my daughter."

"It s not safe to take additional people," they said.

Everything's spinning out of control. All we can do is pray she will make it to the hospital alive. Why didn't the doctors and nurses at this hospital know how to help her? How could they tell me I couldn't be with my daughter? Can this really be happening?

Our only option was to get a grip for long enough to drive the one-and-a-half hours to meet Nikki at the large hospital. We jumped back in the damaged Jeep, numb with fear, and drove as fast as possible. It was a long and arduous trip, but we had no choice.

After about thirty minutes, lights came on behind us, followed by the sound of a siren. How much worse could it get? We have since vowed never to ask that question. To hurry the process of letting the police know why we were speeding, Steve pulled over, jumped out of the Jeep, and ran back toward the police car. Big mistake. (Never do that. They think you're going to attack them.) Fortunately, after they heard our gut-wrenching story, they let us go with a warning to slow down so we wouldn't kill ourselves or anyone else. After driving down many monotonous miles of dark country roads, zoning out on the white center line, once again we spotted a sign with the beautiful blue "H." A few more minutes and we would be with Nikki.

We swerved into the circular driveway of the hospital emergency room and I jumped out before the Jeep came to a complete stop. Rushing over to the main desk, I spilled out my story as fast as I could to the bored-looking receptionist.

Desperate, I asked, "Where can I find her?"

Nonchalantly, the woman checked her records and then looked up at me. "I'm sorry. It looks like you have lost her."

That was more than I could handle. The color drained from my face, my knees buckled under me, and I collapsed to the floor under her counter. She stood looking down at me with a puzzled look on her face.

I was holding my head in my hands, crying. "Oh, my God. She didn't make it."

"Well, honey, I don't know about that, but she must be at the other hospital in town. She's not an admit here."

It took me a few minutes to catch my breath before I stood up, walked to the nearest chair, and sat down.

Steve rushed in, surprised to find me still in the waiting area. I explained that Nikki wasn't there. The receptionist came out from behind her desk and gave us directions to the other hospital, about twenty minutes away. I got up and walked out the door in a daze. Once inside the Jeep, I realized she had absolutely no idea that her answer to my question had been so poorly worded.

Twenty more minutes. Will Nikki make it? Will we make it?

This time, at the correct hospital, we were directed to the Pediatric

ICU. Nikki was still seizing and fighting to stay alive. The doctors had tried multiple cocktails of medications. Nothing was working. Hours went by. How much could her small body take? How many hours could she fight like this? We were totally devastated.

The PICU nurses were going about their business like it was just another day for them. While Nikki was still having violent seizures, one of the nurses complimented me on her cute little pink leather shoes and asked me where I got them. She wanted to find some similar ones for her niece.

My daughter is deathly ill, and this nurse is talking about shoes?

I asked the nurses if they could please just concentrate on helping my daughter.

About 2 a.m., with Nikki still having the seizures, the doctor decided he would have to put her in a medically induced coma. He told us that there were no other options, so we gave our consent. He was right. Her seizures slowly began decreasing until they finally stopped around 4 a.m. For the first time in over ten hours, she was seizure-free. I felt as though I could stop holding my breath, if only for a little while. Nikki seemed to be resting as comfortably as possible given the unfamiliar surroundings. Once we were sure Nikki was stable, we took the hospital staff up on their offer to bring in cots for us, which we immediately fell onto, dirty hunting clothes and all.

How can God let this happen? Why our little girl? Hasn't she been through enough? We know she's a fighter, but give her a break, please.

With these thoughts and prayers coursing through my mind, exhaustion finally took over. We were able to sleep a few hours.

In the morning we called my parents to fill them in and check on Brian. They said he was constantly asking about his baby Nikki and he wanted to see her. Steve and I both felt it would be better for Brian to wait and see her after she was awake. But we had no idea when that would be. My parents had a touchy job ahead of them, keeping Brian distracted while being as honest with him as possible. Thank heavens he had his cousins to play with.

The following day, Nikki was still unconscious, but breathing okay. She was being monitored very closely. We knew we were going to be there for a while, so we checked into the Ronald McDonald House next to the hospital. We didn't have any clean clothes but we were able to shower and brush our teeth. That alone felt like heaven. What a blessing that place was for us. We were also able to have a real sit-down meal. I couldn't remember how long it had been since the last one.

Back at the hospital, Nikki looked small and frail compared to all of the large monitors she was hooked up to. I realized I hadn't been able to hold her since the beginning of this horrendous journey. I asked if it were possible and they hesitantly agreed. I sat down and the nurse very carefully placed her in my arms. She cautioned me to stay very still so as not to dislodge any of Nikki's tubes or disturb her monitors. I sat there motionless quietly staring at her and wondering how long it would be until we could see the sparkle in her eye and her beautiful smile. Then I felt a warm sensation on my leg, and I assumed it was Nikki's diaper leaking. But when I glanced down at the floor, I saw a pool of blood under my feet. I yelled for the nurse, who came and whisked Nikki from my arms to examine her. Somehow, she told me, one of her IV tubes had come out. Once she got her cleaned up she looked fine, but I was too scared to hold her again until all the IV tubes were removed. We spent that day standing by her bed, watching for the flutter of an eye or some sign of movement, even though the doctor told us not to expect any changes for another twenty-four hours. After repeated assurances that Nikki would be monitored closely, we agreed to take a break. After we left her room, we had dinner in the cafeteria and got a full night's sleep.

The next day I asked the doctor, "How are we supposed to live with this time bomb ticking twenty-four hours a day, not knowing when the next seizure will come, how long it will last, and if it will stop on its own? How do I fit this constant unknown into my daily life? Can I still go to work? Can I send her to school? Can I make dinner for my family?"

His simple reply was, "I don't know. You will have to tell me. You and your family will be the ones living this vulnerable and unpredictable life."

How could a doctor say such a thing? Wasn't it common knowledge that doctors had all the answers? Hadn't this been embedded into our culture? Weren't they the experts we could lean on whenever a medical problem occurred? Now what? This was a scary realization.

We were on our own with this. If the doctor didn't know the answers, how could we? After thinking about it for a while, I wondered why I ever could have expected a doctor to have all the answers. This was a unique situation that few members of the medical profession had experienced first-hand. How could any of them possibly know everything there was to know in every given situation? In some cases, they were learning along with their patients. Maybe that was why they called it "practicing" medicine.

This incident was yet another turning point for me. I had learned that there is no exact answer in medicine—nor necessarily a track record to rely on. Plus, new information is coming to light every day, which calls into question the advice you were given yesterday.

The next day, the plan was for my parents to bring Brian to see Nikki, and to bring us some clean clothes. Nikki was showing brief signs of waking and most of the tubes had been removed. We hoped she wouldn't look too sick for Brian.

When they arrived, I found myself desperately needing a Brian hug, which was the best medicine I could have asked for. He handled seeing Nikki in the hospital like a trooper, as it was not a totally new experience for him. We told him that she was getting better every day, and we would be bringing her back to camp very soon. After a few hours, Brian was content to go back and play with his cousins.

Nikki remained in the hospital for five long days. What we didn't know was how much brain damage those ten hours of seizures might have caused. On the last day, she was standing up in her crib. We saw that sparkle in her eyes again and that beautiful crooked smile.

She had made it! We had made it! We didn't know how long she would be okay, but does anybody ever really know? We were going home, back to the uncharted territory of raising Nikki.

WE ARE GOING TO BE OK

One of Nikki's favorite things in life has always been food. At an early age, she learned to seek out the golden arches of McDonald's. Why not? They equaled a Happy Meal and a delicious chocolate milkshake—a special treat that was known to put a smile on her face and make her tummy happy.

For her third birthday, we decided to take her to her happy place to celebrate. This wouldn't have been our first choice for a birthday dinner, however, it wasn't our birthday!

Nikki's eyes were wide with anticipation as I put her food in front of her. She moved her meal in a little closer and looked over at us like she had something on her mind. Usually when food was within arm's reach, the green light would go on and there was no coming up for air until not a single morsel was left. This time was different. It seemed she had a strategic plan that required her to keep an eye on us and our food. Then, at an opportune moment, her little arm jetted out to our trays to snatch a french fry or two from under our noses. We signed "no" to her and then got on with our meals.

Even as she slowly began eating her own meal, Nikki continued sneaking in her little klepto moments. For the first time ever, we finished eating before she did. When she realized all our food was gone, that's when she got on with finishing her own, giggling with every gulp.

The little trickster! Who said she was slow? She was able to outwit all of us, and she did so with total glee. Her happiness and giggles were contagious, and soon we were all laughing.

That was when it dawned on me. I had been reading about the seven stages of grief, and it was what we had been experiencing since Nikki's birth. Shock and denial were behind us, as were pain and guilt, anger and bargaining, depression, reflection, and loneliness. It had required all of our strength, love, and commitment, but we now felt we were on the upturn. We could finally reach that illusive top step of appreciation on the healing ladder we had long been climbing, one rung at a time. It was during that simple dinner that we moved into the appreciation stage. What a great feeling it was to realize that, as a family, we had been able to move upwards and put some of the hard times behind us. We could just accept the uniqueness of Nikki's life and learn to appreciate every moment. At that particular moment, things seemed pretty darn good.

Day in and day out, Nikki would continue to remind us of her uniqueness and, even at times, her comic quirky tendencies. To discover the things in life that Nikki truly loves has always made us happy. We adore her innocence and the joy she gets from simple pleasures. Her joy is infectious. Once you've caught the Nikki bug, there is no going back. She asks for very little and gives so much back to everyone around her.

Some of her favorite toys, which we call her "squigglies," were snakes, lizards, and iguanas...the wigglier and slimier, the better. Once, when we were walking out of the hospital after another routine blood test, I noticed that people were jumping out of our way with odd looks on their faces. I couldn't imagine what was wrong with them until I looked down at Nikki. In her mouth, she had the head of her long iguana, which she was whipping back and forth with a devious smile on her face. You had to love her.

Second only to her squigglies were her favorite flowers that we call her "twirlies." For some strange reason, Nikki loved the long-stemmed weeds with the bright yellow flowers better than any others for her twirling pleasure. Maybe it was the roundness of the stems that fit so perfectly between her fingers as she rolled them back and forth. Who knows for sure? Whatever it was, it worked out well since, whenever we took walks, she wouldn't be asking me to pick flowers from our neighbor's well manicured gardens. She would only focus on those twirlies far ahead of us. When I picked one for her, her smile would just blossom.

After long days with her squigglies and twirlies, Nikki would be ready for her other favorite part of the day—her tubby. Oh, how she loves her bubble baths! The comfort of the warm water, the mounds of bubbles to flick, and the buoyancy of her body in the water—that was Nikki's definition

of heaven on earth. Sometimes she would want to stay in the bathwater for hours. As she lingered, the bubbles would begin to dissipate and her water would cool down. Nikki would let me know in her own way that this was not okay. She had learned on her own how to turn on the faucet to warm up the water—both a blessing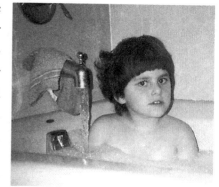

and a curse. However, she still had to point out to me whenever there was a lack of bubbles so I would rebuild her bubble bank. We would have to stay right there with her the entire time to make sure she didn't overflow the tub or start making her own kind of bath toys. Invariably, after her long tubby, she would be in a gleeful mood and would do her "happy hop" down the hallway. Her unique brand of walking has always been a sure sign to us that she was in a happy and contented mood. How we love to see her happy hop! Step, hop…step, hop…step, hop! It always reminded us of the beloved actor Walter Brennan, whom we've enjoyed in so many classic movies.

Nikki also loves massages and anything that vibrates against her skin. She likes having her head massaged and her hair brushed. Once, I found a vibrating hairbrush that was a big hit with her. She also loves having the underside of her arms massaged with gentle strokes, using lotions or lightweight brushes. Another favorite indulgence is having her feet rubbed. Whenever we were in the car during her childhood, Nikki would stick her feet up from the back seat onto the front seat armrests. This was our cue that she wanted her shoes taken off and her feet rubbed. We also discovered she enjoyed joint compression, which helped calm her down. Whenever we discovered something new that would make her happy, we made sure she continued to have it on a regular basis: squigglies, twirlies, tubbies, massages, mirrors, and all.

Nikki also loves pigs: stuffed pigs, photos of pigs, real pigs…you name it. One of Nikki's daycare providers would take Nikki to the county fair specifically to see the pigs. The highlight was visiting the tent where 4-H members were showing off their prize pigs. After making the mistake of momentarily taking her eyes off Nikki to greet a friend, she turned back around only to find Nikki gone. Then suddenly she heard that telltale squeal of delight. She turned around to see Nikki inside the pigpen hugging the prizewinner.

One Halloween, at a pumpkin patch, Nikki spotted her favorite animal, a large pot-bellied pig running around loose. She was watching it very intently. Then the next thing we knew, she was trying to climb on its back to ride it. Giddy-up, Porky!

✦ ✦ ✦

It seems that Nikki's uniqueness has been contagious and has had a trickle-down effect on our entire family. We were all the better for having caught it early in life. She has taught us to enjoy the moment for what it is, no matter how unique it might be.

One Easter Sunday, we were dressed up in our Easter finest, ready to go. First came Easter brunch, followed by the community Easter egg hunt. We arrived at the park, baskets in hand. Brian was brimming with excitement as Steve took him to the section for his five-year-old age group, while Nikki and I went to hers. As we walked along, I pointed out an egg and helped her, hand over hand, put it in her basket. We did this a few more times, but she was clearly not interested. All she wanted to do was sit down in the sun and play with her twirlies. As long as she could feel the warmth on her back while twirling her flower she was happy, and that's what mattered.

It wasn't long before Brian came running to us, squealing with delight. After finding the golden egg, he grinned from ear to ear as he showed Nikki his treasure, knowing she would be proud of him. They walked together, hand in hand, to turn in the glittery egg for an Easter basket full of goodies. A true triumph for the day.

Now it was time to go home and play in the backyard while we did some gardening. Once we got home, I noticed that Nikki's hearing aids were missing. I knew I had put them in that day. Where could they be? First, I checked the car, but no luck. Okay, we knew what we had to do—retrace our steps, especially because these were so expensive and this was already her second pair. We all climbed back in the car and set off. First, to the restaurant. Nope. Then off to the park where the Easter egg hunt had been. There we were, after everyone else had gone, starting our second Easter egg hunt of the day. We gave Brian his basket again, trying to make it fun, and searched the area where Nikki and I had been. I had never realized how many hiding places there were in a field. It took some time, but finally I noticed something familiar - the hearing aides - in a patch of sour grass. Hallelujah! Two successful Easter egg hunts in one day.

✦ ✦ ✦

Brian continued to show his genuine compassion for his little sister through his loving actions, even in the middle of the night. It was after midnight and I had just gotten Nikki to sleep. Brian had already been asleep for hours, all tucked in with his loyal puppy, Daisy. It was time to do all the daily chores that had to be put on hold during Nikki's nighttime routine. As I sat down to write checks, I realized that there were more bills than money—something that was happening more and more often. In my pre-panic frustration, I remembered that Nikki's seizure medications were ready to be picked up at the pharmacy. How was I going to do that considering there was nothing left in the bank balance after paying that last dreaded bill?

I went to brainstorm with Steve, who was working at the computer. What options did we have to pay for these much-needed seizure medications? The only thing we could come up with was to charge them on the credit card. I didn't like that option, as it went against my goal to reduce our credit card debt.

Just then, I heard some movement from the darkness of Brian s bedroom. Next, I heard the jingling of Daisy's collar as Brian poked his head out of his bedroom door. There he was in his little one-piece Superman PJs, hair rumpled, with his trusty sidekick, Daisy.

"Brian, I thought you were asleep, I said.

"I was, but now I'm not," he said. "I want to give you something."

What? At this time of night?

"I think this could help you," he said.

Then I saw his little fist open up like a flower, and there, in the palm of his hand was his hand-painted tooth fairy box. "I have been saving my toof money for something I really want, and I want Nikki to have her see-zure pills."

Tears welled up in my eyes as I reached down and hugged him

tightly. I felt so much love that it hurt. Even though times were tough raising Nikki, right then I felt we must be doing something right. To have a son
who was so caring, compassionate and unselfish at such a young age was a
blessing we never took for granted. There was no Superman in the world
any more super than Brian!

✦ ✦ ✦

Life adventures along the way with Nikki have taught us to find the
humor in some of our more out-of-the-ordinary moments, of which there
were many. Since these experiences were our new normal, we had plenty of
opportunities to laugh. This adventure would be no different.

The evening before we were to leave for another family hunting trip, I
planned to finish up the last minute details so we could all get a good night's
sleep. We wanted to be bright and rested to get an early morning start on
our adventure.

I was finishing up the food preparation for the trip, washing clothes,
packing, cooking dinner, and getting Nikki ready for bed, all at the same
time. Multi-tasking had become my way of life. Steve had taken Brian with
him to run the final errands. I was bouncing back and forth between the
bathroom, where Nikki was in the tub, the living room, where I was folding
the last load of towels, and the kitchen, where I was packaging up a large
pot of bean soup I had made for the trip. As I was leaving the kitchen, I
turned on the oven to preheat, so I could warm up the leftovers we were
going to have for dinner.

When I got back to the bathroom, Nikki had somehow turned her ele-
phant-head protective shower hose backwards, and it was siphoning the tub
water onto the floor. UGH! Fortunately, I had a pile of clean towels close
by to soak up the inches of water covering the bathroom floor. So much for
almost having all the laundry done. Once I had Nikki out of the tub and
into her pink pajamas, she toddled out to the living room where she liked to
curl up on the couch. I went back to collect the soaked towels and headed to

the laundry room. When I went back to the living room, there was no Nikki, but I saw smoke billowing out of the kitchen accompanied by a strong, rancid odor. I ran to the kitchen and stopped in my tracks.

There was Nikki sitting in the middle of the floor, covered from head to toe with soupy beans. She was smiling as she flicked beans into the air, some of which stuck to the walls. Daisy was happily licking her face while slipping and sliding in the mess. I realized she must have found the pot of cooled soup that I had left on the kitchen counter to pack for the trip and decided to investigate. Now, the smoke alarm started blaring. I could see smoke oozing out from the oven door. I dropped the dripping towels and ran to the oven. When I opened the oven door, the hot smoke hit me in the face. Through the haze, I could see something that looked like a pair of boots. When I looked closer I was shocked to see Brian's first pair of big boy leather hunting boots–the ones we had just bought him for the trip. I pulled them out and saw that the leather soles were curled up like potato chips. They were definitely well done.

Right then Steve and Brian entered the smoke-filled, smelly kitchen. As they stepped over the mound of wet towels, they saw me holding the smoking boots. Then, they noticed Nikki and Daisy covered in bean soup. The look on Brian's face was one of pure horror. The smoke alarm underscored his uncontrollable sobbing.

After getting over the initial shock, Steve offered a full confession loud enough that I could hear it over the alarm. "All I did was waterproof them, and then put them into the oven. I thought the pilot light would dry them before we left."

"Very inventive of you, but next time you're planning to do this, give me a heads-up so I won't preheat the oven for dinner."

After the smoke cleared and the alarm stopped blaring, the total absurdity of the situation hit us. Steve and I burst out laughing. Nikki and Daisy were still having fun. But Brian, with his beautiful boots gone up in smoke, saw no humor in it at all. To this day, he doesn't recall the situation as having been remotely funny. I, on the other hand, will never forget the sight of Nikki and Daisy sitting on the kitchen floor, covered in bean soup, oblivious to the smoke and the smell of Brian's brand new boots baking in the oven.

That memory is always good for a laugh. The next day, we managed to leave on our trip, but not as early as planned, and we were nowhere near close to being rested. Even after a less than perfect beginning, the trip ended up being a success.

Some of our adventures went far less smoothly, but we never gave up trying. The first trip we took to the mountains with Steve's family, unfortunately, was one of those. They had always taken an annual post-Thanksgiving ski trip to the Sierras. Nikki was usually sick at this time of year and we had never been able to go. As her immune system seemed to get stronger as she got older, we wanted to give it a try. I knew the altitude could affect the seizure threshold for some people, however I also knew that every person was different.

We decided to think positive and embark on another adventure. As we drove and the altitude increased, we kept a close eye on Nikki. Just as we arrived at the cabin, she began seizing. Our hearts sank, especially Brian's. We got her inside, hoping this might be a short series of seizures before she acclimated to the higher elevation. We waited and watched for over forty-five minutes, but no luck. Her seizures were getting longer and more intense. All we could do was get her down off the mountain. We worked it out so Brian could stay, and Steve's parents would drive him home after the weekend. Steve and I drove down the mountain toward home with Nikki.

Within twenty minutes, the seizures had stopped completely.

Even though we were relieved, the long trip home was very quiet.

✦ ✦ ✦

As Christmas drew closer, I still felt some disappointment over our failed family outing to the mountains. A friend at work mentioned he had taken his kids to a Christmas tree farm about forty-five minutes away, where they were able to cut down their own Christmas tree. He said there was snow on the ground, Christmas music playing in the background, and an abundance of refreshments awaiting their return from their tree hunt. That sounded perfect. I could already visualize it and smell the fresh pine trees, as I relived my childhood memories of Christmas tree hunting.

That evening, with the Christmas tree farm in mind, I imposed my power of persuasion on Steve. "Maybe we can regain some of our lost family time and begin a new tradition of our own."

"Excellent idea. Let's do it."

The following Saturday, off we went in search of our tree. The kids got to wear their new snow clothes and excitement was in the air. We loaded up the van and headed out, listening to Christmas music as we drove.

Upon our arrival at the farm, we were confused by the contrast between what had been described to us and what we actually saw. Worst of all, there were no acres of trees as I was used to seeing in Oregon. After we drove through a gate and onto a dirt road, we noticed some frost on the ground, but no trace of snow. Had the temperature warmed up a lot in the previous few days and melted everything? At the end of the road, we saw an old trailer with a carport and a man standing outside. I got out of the car to ask him for directions to the tree farm.

He said, "You're here, ma'am."

"What? Well, where are the Christmas trees? I asked.

"Only have a few out back," he said.

As I turned back to the car, I shot Steve a look of total confusion.

I told the kids, "All righty, then. I guess we're here."

Country-western music was blasting out of the owner's dusty little boom box. Was that the background Christmas music I had heard about?

"What happened to the snow?" I asked.

"Oh, don't get much of that white stuff up here…mostly just frost."

Had my friend been delusional, or was he just not used to real snow?

The man showed us the small patch of Christmas trees behind his trailer, and we went back there with our saw in hand. It was too warm to wear all the snow clothes we brought, so everyone began shedding layers into my outstretched arms. In the end, the tree we selected was far from what we had anticipated, but we decided it was ours. We cut it down, hauled it to the van, and strapped it to the top.

Now for the refreshments. As we walked back to the carport, we saw a table with a Crock-Pot filled with cocktail-size weenies in ketchup sauce and a few cans of soda. Steve looked at me, and all I could do was smile and shrug my shoulders. Even though it wasn't the elaborate spread I had imagined—not even close—the kids enjoyed it. On the way home, listening to Christmas music on the car radio, we planned how we would decorate our tree.

I'm still not sure if this was a case of exaggeration or too high expectations, or maybe a bit of both. I reminded Steve that all of these memories would only get better with time.

✦ ✦ ✦

Our next trip took us north to Oregon to visit my family. Everyone loved these visits, especially Grandma Eva, who always looked forward to our arrival and welcomed us with open arms. She was my mom's mom, my grandma, and great-grandma to Brian and Nikki. A beautiful, kind-hearted woman, she absolutely adored her great-grandchildren. Steve and I were okay too, but in no way a match for them. After a bad fall in her late forties, she became physically disabled and went through a series of debilitating back surgeries. Although her injuries left her in constant pain whether she was sitting or walking, she kept a positive attitude and unfaltering faith. She simply found joy in those basic activities she could do lying down. One of her favorite pastimes was lying on the bed with Nikki by her side.

They cuddled, played patty-cake, and did the chin-tap game – all the things that Nikki loved to do. Although Nikki was deaf, Grandma Eva would sing to her. In turn, Nikki would express her delight by giggling and clapping!

Those were special times. Grandma was happy and Nikki was happy. It was beautiful to watch as they built their beautiful relationship and radiated in the pleasure of each other's company. I would check on them periodically until Grandma Eva got tired of telling me, "We're fine. Go do your thing."

That was my cue to take a break and visit other family members.

During these visits, Grandma Eva felt she had a purpose, and Nikki knew she had a very special friend and ally. Although it was usually months between visits, whenever we were there, it felt as though no time had passed for Grandma Eva and Nikki.

When we received the dreadful news that Grandma Eva had been diagnosed with an aggressive form of cancer, we immediately made arrangements to go see her. Spending time with Nikki seemed to be her most powerful medicine. On that visit, she gave me a jade butterfly necklace which she said reminded her of Nikki, who was "as beautiful as a butterfly."

Weeks after Grandma Eva's funeral service, Nikki and I were home enjoying a sunny fall afternoon on the front porch. We were doing the chin-tapping game and playing patty-cake. The birds were singing and we were warmed by the sun's healing rays. It was a day of total contentment and joy. Out of nowhere came a beautiful monarch butterfly, fluttering just inches away from us before landing on Nikki's knee as she sat cross-legged, her favorite sitting pose. At first, she leaned forward to get a closer look at the butterfly, and then she leaned back and started to clap her hands. As I watched in utter amazement, I noticed the little creature wasn't scared off by the clapping. Rather, it remained fixed to Nikki's knee for some time before finally flying away.

Although I will never really know what took place in that fleeting moment, I will always have my theory. I've found that some things cannot be explained with logic, so it's best to let the heart figure them out. And my heart keeps reminding me that Nikki will always have a special connection with Grandma Eva, regardless of the boundaries separating heaven and earth. To this day, I can still hear Grandma Eva saying, "Anything can happen. Remember, they said Nikki wasn't going to make it."

PART TWO
✦
NIKKI: AGE 3 - 5

NIKKI GOES TO SCHOOL

A new chapter in our lives was about to begin when Nikki was three years old and September was approaching. It was time for her to enter the world of school. I knew it was going to be difficult for me to adjust, but since Nikki was growing up, it was time for me to do the same. Also, it was financially necessary for me to get back to my part-time job on a more regular basis. What we didn't realize was that there was an extreme shortage of educational opportunities for children with multiple challenges.

It had always been easy for us to know which school and classroom Brian would be attending. Unfortunately, it wasn't as easy to find the proper placement for Nikki. The options were few and far between, with none in our local district. Since Nikki was deaf, her classroom options were even more limited. I had heard great things about a primary grade special education class for hearing-impaired students that was just twenty minutes away. I was hoping she'd be accepted. The main concern on the part of the school was that Nikki was also developmentally delayed. Would she fit in? Would she slow the education process for the others in class?

We had a meeting with about twelve representatives of the powers-that-be to see if we could all come to an agreement that this class should be Nikki's first placement. I suggested, this seemed like the best option and the Least Restrictive Environment (LRE) for her. LRE is a term I had learned by researching how to get the best education for a disabled child. Using the right terminology helped me get Nikki a unanimous vote for this class placement.

The teachers were great and they did everything they could to help Nikki succeed. But it was a struggle since most of her hearing-impaired classmates seemed to have normal processing abilities. Over the course of the school year, however, a few other students in her class were found to have multiple disabilities. That laid the groundwork for approval to start a new class specifically for hearing-impaired students with multiple disabilities. This new classroom seemed like a perfect fit for Nikki. At first she was able to progress, as her teacher became another of her strong advocates. He was a great teacher and we developed a close friendship with him. But when Nikki began a series of medication changes due to her seizures, her behavior became increasingly difficult to deal with. Her teacher was forced to recommend we look for other placement options for her the following year. I tried not to take it personally, but it still hurt.

Not sure where to turn, I called the behavior specialist, Vicci Tucci, with whom we had been working at home on some of Nikki's challenging behaviors. She highly recommended a teacher named Debbie, who had a special education class in a school in Salinas which was even farther away. We set up a time to meet and I loved Debbie immediately. I didn't like the idea of my little girl spending two hours each way on a bus every day. However, knowing she would be in good hands, I agreed that this was the best placement option available for her.

The next September, Nikki started at her new school in Salinas, and wouldn't you know, she loved the longer bus rides. In fact, they may have been her favorite part of the day. Obviously, it was a lot easier on her than it was on me. Nikki not only liked her new class and her teacher, she also began participating more in both group and individual activities. She even learned some basic sign language and could communicate some of her wants and needs.

In our daily communication notebooks, Debbie reported that Nikki was calm and happy at school. At home, however, she began wreaking havoc. She would climb up on our bed and try to knock the framed pictures off the wall. If she got to them before I could get to her, many of them fell and broke. She also seemed to have an aversion to lamps, having broken all of them in the house within a one-month time period.

Why is she doing this? Is she punishing me because she would rather be at school? What am I doing wrong?

I got to the point where I was frustrated beyond belief and enough was enough. I called Vicci Tucci again and anxiously waited for her to check her schedule. She could come see us in a week. "In the meantime," she said, "you will have to jump through some more bureaucratic hoops to make it happen."

I was getting used to this by now, and I had a week to deal with forms, waivers, phone calls, and getting the visit approved. Once again hope was on the horizon. The next week went by slowly, while Nikki continued to break anything breakable in her path. Lamps were no longer a problem as we had put in all recessed lighting. Still, she would climb up on the furniture in search of framed pictures to knock down.

When Vicci arrived, I ran out to greet her, alerting her that Nikki was still up to her shenanigans. "Please help me. I'm running out of options."

Vicci smiled, entered the house and greeted Nikki. Then she turned to me and said, "If it's okay with you, I would like to be left alone with her for a while. I'd like to observe her in action."

She didn't have to tell me twice. "Take as much time as you need. I'll be in the van in the driveway taking a much-needed nap."

Since I was constantly in a sleep-deprived state, I had developed the ability to nap anytime, anywhere, as long as I didn't have to listen for Nikki. I had been known to fall asleep in the car or the bathtub, or on the cold, hard floor; it didn't matter where, as long as I could close my eyes and rest. And that was what I was doing in the van. It seemed like no time at all before I heard a soft tapping on the window. I opened my eyes and saw a smiling face peering in at me.

"Come in here. You need to see this."

I followed Vicci into the house. Nikki was standing on our bed with her hands all over the pictures.

"Look closely. What is she really looking at?" she asked me.

"The picture," I said.

"Get closer."

Bewildered, I got up on the bed with Nikki and stared into the same picture that had caught her attention. I finally saw what she'd been looking at. "Her reflection?" I asked.

"Exactly. She's not trying to break things. She's not trying to punish you. All she wants is a mirror. She likes looking at her reflection."

Vicci explained that the school classroom had mirrors placed low along the walls because the students enjoyed making faces at themselves and observing their reflections. "It's a natural part of her development. It's just coming a little later for her."

Then I made a confession to Vicci. "All this time I was thinking uncontrollable, negative thoughts about my own daughter. And now I realize that I'm the one at fault. Why can't I slow down enough to put myself in her shoes and really listen to her needs?"

"Because you're her mom," she said sternly. "You have so much on your plate, it's nearly impossible to be objective. Do yourself a long overdue favor. Give yourself a break." Looking at me with a smirk on her face, she added, "Now go and buy your daughter a damned mirror."

That's exactly what I did. Since that day, Nikki has not broken a single lamp or picture. Her small mirrors are some of her favorite things and they probably always will be. She has a wide assortment of them and we plan to keep it that way. We have all learned the hard way to never leave home without one.

✦ ✦ ✦

During these pre-school years, Nikki began having more frequent bouts of crying and increased signs of agitation and aggression. Yet, she hadn't shown any signs of illness, and her seizure meds had been fairly consistent for a while. I couldn't figure out what had changed and I was concerned she might be in pain. It was never far from my mind that she might be developing tumor-like growths in her vital organs.

Around this time, our pediatrician learned that a new pediatric neurologist had started to practice locally and he recommended that we meet him. He knew we had always been forced to travel long distances on a regular basis for Nikki's appointments and thought this would make life so much easier. After an initial consultation, the doctor agreed to accept Nikki as a patient. He was knowledgeable in his field but seemed quite aloof.

He's smart and he's local. Two out of three isn't bad.

Things went fairly well for a while. He worked with us through hospital visits for pneumonia, status epilepticus, and the many trial-and-error stints with different seizure meds, daily blood level checks, and all the associated side effects.

For all of our appointments with the neurologist, Brian, who was a little over five at the time, asked to go with me. He always wanted to know how he could help his little sister. During my next scheduled appointment, I expressed my concerns to the doctor about the recent changes in Nikki's behavior and my worry about the possibilities of tubers in her brain. He quickly alleviated that concern since she was not presenting the classic symptoms: lethargy and vomiting.

"Okay. Then what else could it be? I asked.

That was when he lowered the boom on me and began his shocking monologue. "If she were my daughter, I would use a cattle prod on her. You have to come to grips with the fact that her mind is like an empty black box. She can't show or understand any emotions or pain." Just as I was about to interrupt him and defend Nikki, he held up his hand to silence me. Then, he continued his tirade. "What you should do is empty a dark closet and put a lock on the outside of it." Then he turned to Brian, to involve him in the plan. "You could play policeman and, whenever your little sister begins to act up and cry, you could put her in the dark closet and lock it. Then you can make her stay in there until she quiets down."

The doctor continued. "By doing this, you could earn tokens, which your mommy could put toward buying you your favorite toys. How does that sound?"

Brian looked hurt and confused and I was merely speechless, desperate to get the hell out of there. I grabbed Brian's hand and all together we walked out of the office without saying a word. I vowed never go back to him.

Years later, as Nikki's seizures and behavior became more intense due to the complications of hormones, I had to eat my words and go back to that neurologist. I needed his knowledge of medication options. It was only for Nikki's sake that I decided to put up with his rudeness. For a short while, we worked together again. Our last telephone conversation ended with him telling me, "Shit or get off the pot." This was definately a new medical term I had not heard before. This sobering experience made me wonder if neurologists in general were a breed apart, or if I had merely been unlucky.

✦ ✦ ✦

Our plans for family outings and other activities were always made in the hope of creating some semblance of normalcy within our abnormal lives. I found that trying to fit the proverbial square peg into the round hole seldom worked out as planned, but I refused to be beaten. All I could do was prepare for Nikki's needs in each case and pray for the best possible outcome.

I had made plans for the kids and me to spend the weekend with my friend and her daughter. With more than two hours of driving ahead of us, the goal was to leave as soon as I got home from work. The day got off to a good start, as Nikki had slept pretty well the night before. She woke up in good spirits and was still in a happy mood when we put her on the school bus. After taking Brian to school, I began packing...rather over-packing. Once everything was in the van, it looked as though we expected to be gone for weeks rather than a couple of days. Then I drove to my office.

I was just beginning my workday, reviewing my agenda, when I got a call from Nikki' s teacher.

Uh-oh. That's never a good sign.

Always anticipating the next seizure time bomb, my heart started speeding up. "Does she have a fever? Is she getting sick? Is she seizing?"

I held my breath, waiting for an answer. The teacher assured me that wasn't the case. However, there was something wrong. Nikki was crying, kicking and bashing her forehead against the walls. She had even kicked over a desk.

"No one can calm her down," she said. "You'll have to come get her."

By this time, I knew the drill. Drop everything and run. I needed to get to Nikki right away despite the fact that I had an important advertising meeting that afternoon. Normally, it wouldn't have been that big of a deal, but on that particular day, I was scheduled to present a proposal that I had been working on for weeks. With no other option, I would just have to follow our family motto, Adapt and Adjust, a line of reasoning that Brian hates to this day. As I drove to the school, my mind started taking me places I didn't want to go. Once I was outside of Nikki's classroom, I could hear the pain in her voice as it trailed into the hallway. Knowing that she was hurting truly made me sick inside. She had gone through so much already with no end in sight.

Because of her delayed development and deafness, she was not able to tell us where it hurt. It was always a guessing game. When I picked her up in my arms and tried to console her, I was almost in tears. She seemed to quiet down for a few minutes, but then she started crying and kicking again. None of us knew what to do to take away the hurt she was feeling. One of the worst feelings imaginable for a parent is knowing their child is in agony and being helpless to alleviate it.

My mind was racing as I got Nikki into the car. Then I called Lynn, who was Nikki's and Brian's after-school caregiver. I explained the situation to her and asked for her advice. She said she was free that morning and suggested I bring Nikki to her home. Since she had a knack with her and knew she could calm her down, I decided to take her there just long enough for me to get through my meeting.

Okay, now I had a plan. It was a sressful drive but Nikki seemed to be quieting down some as we drove. The car always had a calming effect on her. When we arrived, Lynn came out to the car to get her and found me just as worked up as Nikki.

"How can I go to work when my little one is in so much pain? What kind of mother am I?"

"Oh, for God's sake! Get off your pity pot and go to work. She'll be fine."

After a few deep breaths, I was on my way back to work. I made it to the meeting—barely—but I would be lying if I said that I was relaxed and composed. I did get through my presentation and, when it was over and all of the handshaking was done, I ran to the phone and called Lynn. At that point, I was hoping for some good news, but that wasn't the case. Nikki was still inconsolable. Maybe she was constipated, I thought, as some of her seizure meds were known to have that effect. Whatever the problem, my workday was over and I was on my way to collect Nikki and Brian, who I knew could make her smile.

By the time I arrived at Lynn's, Nikki was playing with Brian and seemed better. We left directly from there on our trip. Brian promised to keep his sister entertained in the backseat. We would stop for dinner on the way down, after which Nikki would surely have a bowel movement and life would get back to our version of normal.

As we began the drive, Brian was able to calm Nikki down. But after about forty-five minutes, she began wailing and kicking again. I decided to take off her shoes and socks, as I knew that massaging her feet always helped her relax. With one hand on the steering wheel, I used the other to take off one shoe and then the other. Next, I grabbed the top rib of one sock and started to pull it off, but it was stuck and refused to budge. That was when Nikki screamed like I had never heard her scream before. What was wrong? When I tried again to take off her sock, I found something inside it was attached to her toe. We had to help her and it had to be fast. I told Brian to hold her hand while I got us off the freeway. We were only one exit away from a McDonald's, Nikki's favorite place, so I raced there, parked, and ran her inside. We needed to see what was going on, causing her the indescribable pain that she had been enduring for the past eight hours.

And there it was, revealed at last. The string inside the top seam of one of her socks had somehow gotten tied around her big toe. Once we were able to break the string, she immediately smiled and signed for her dinner. The crisis was over, but I was still a basket case. Her injured toe was a deep shade of blue, encircled by an ashen gray line of dead skin tissue. How could we all have missed this? We thought we had checked everything. Brian and I were both speechless, but Nikki was just hungry.

It took months for the circulation in her toe to come back. Eventually, the dead tissue dried up and sloughed off. But, my memory of the experience remained. What did we learn that day? When Nikki shows pain, we have to be prepared, literally, to strip her from head to toe.

✦ ✦ ✦

When Nikki's preschool years were coming to a close, the school-placement search for Nikki was back on. Debbie went with me to observe her available options. Unfortunately, nothing seemed like a good fit. I discussed the meager possibilities with our school district's special education coordinator, Doug Brown. He asked me, "What do you feel would be the perfect scenario for her?"

The question caught me off guard. "Yeah, like that's ever going to happen,"

"No, really. Think about it," he insisted. "You don't get if you don't ask."

It didn't take me long to come up with an answer. "Okay. I want a class to open in our local school district and I know exactly which teacher I want: Debbie Thomas."

He said, "Sounds good. Let me see what I can do."

I never understood how he did it, but that exact class eventually opened and Debbie was happy to relocate nearby. The school embraced the class, as did all of the participating families. It felt like nothing short of a miracle.

✦ ✦ ✦

As Nikki was turning five, along with everything else, the cost of her diapers was really adding up. I mentioned this to the parent of another disabled child and her response surprised me.

"Why are you paying for them? Diapers are a product that our regional center should be covering. They have been paying for my son's diapers since he turned two. He's eight years old now."

"Why didn't anyone tell me?" I asked. "They come to my house for meetings at least twice a year and we talk on the phone at least once a month."

"Did you ever ask them specifically if they would pay for Nikki's diapers?"

"Well, no. I thought they would tell me which products and services were available and what Nikki qualified for."

"Unfortunately, it doesn't work like that."

I called my caseworker, and she agreed that this was an expense they covered. She would set up monthly deliveries for me.

"Why didn't you ever mention this to me over these past three years?"

"I'm instructed never to offer anything unless I'm asked specifically. It's a way of keeping costs down."

"That's a little unfair, don't you think?

"If I had offered it to you on my own, I could have lost my job."

And these were our advocates? This was a very important lesson to be learned early on.

For me, it was a case of better late than never.

LIVING OUR LIVES, ONE DAY AT A TIME

Life isn't about waiting for the showers to pass...
It s about learning to dance in the rain.
Vivian Greene

❖ ❖ ❖

O ur daily life was complicated to say the least. We never had much
time or energy to compare our family with others. We just kept putting one foot in front of the other to make our lives work.

Early on, we learned to accept the fact that, for us, the normal frustra-
tions that came with raising children would be multiplied and amplified ac-
cordingly. It seemed that things went wrong more often, more dramatically,
and the problems lasted longer. We expanded our concept of "normal."
Some snippets of family experiences with our own Gould-style twist follow:

❖ ❖ ❖

With all that we had on our plate due to Nikki's multiple disabilities,
sleep deprivation caused the most havoc in our daily lives. I should have
realized that sleep was going to be a lifelong problem for Nikki when she
was still in her crib. Night after night, when I put her to bed, she would cry
herself into a frenzy until she got worked up and sweaty.

The doctors kept reminding me: "Tough love, Jeanie. You need to let
her cry herself to sleep."

This was always a lot harder with her than it was with Brian. I was
afraid she would work herself into a seizure. I tried to do what the doctors
recommended although, sometimes, when I was ready to give in to her,

Steve had to hold me back. One night, Nikki was exceptionally wound up and wailing. It was killing me not to go to her. Then I heard a loud thud in her room, followed by a hold-your-breath kind of silence. Frantically, I ran to her room and switched on the light. There was Nikki, face down on the floor and she was not moving. When I picked her up, her eyes were as big as saucers. The wind had been knocked out of her. I was thankful to see that a large pillow on the floor had cushioned her fall. Either her aim was excellent or she was very lucky.

When she outgrew her crib, we discovered that Nikki liked to sleep in small, enclosed spaces, so we put a Little Tyke Cottage, complete with a cushiony foam mattress, in the bedroom that she shared with Brian. He slept in his big-boy bed alongside her. This is when he learned how to sleep through almost anything. Then, when both kids were older, we turned our office into a room for Nikki. We quickly realized she didn't sleep well alone, so night after night, I would lay with her for hours, waiting for her to fall asleep. To make sure I couldn't get up to leave, she would twist me into her favorite pretzel position. Then, once I was certain she was asleep, I would move ever so slowly, a few inches at a time, attempting to get out of her bed without waking her. I knew that if she awoke, I would have to start the entire process all over again.

Whenever we went on vacations with other family members, we hoped some of them would volunteer to sleep with Nikki. Initially, most of them loved the idea of spending that much quality time with her. However, once they actually experienced it, they came up with a lot of creative excuses. Usually, with no one else volunteering, Steve or I ended up taking on the task. If we couldn't get Nikki to sleep, we had to confine her to our room so she wouldn't wake everyone else. Even though we barricaded the door with furniture or other large objects, somehow, she would make her way around them and tug at the door.

Sometimes on these family trips we would have to double-team her. My mom and I would lie down on either side of Nikki, praying she would eventually fall asleep. We each had a leg intertwined pretzel-style with hers, and we were each rubbing one of her inner arms, which always seemed to help her relax. After she went through a few acrobatic moves, we would resume massaging her arms. One time, we had a good laugh when my mom got confused about whose arm was whose, and she ended up massaging my arm instead of Nikki's. "Oh, Mom," I said, "that feels so good."

We tried every sleep supplement we could find for her, even a rare Chinese herb we could only purchase in San Francisco's Chinatown. They each worked for a while, and then they would lose their effectiveness. Once, I was so desperate that, in my exhausted stupor, I prayed for someone—anyone—to come to the door and agree to watch Nikki for just two hours. I was truly prepared to pay $500 for a sampling of uninterrupted sleep.

Oh, precious sleep, worth more than gold...

I would always dread the time when Nikki needed a haircut. We purposely kept her hair short for easy maintenance, so she needed them all too often. I tried having her hair done professionally but more often than not, it was a recipe for disaster. On rare occasions, she would sit quietly. Other times, not so much. Over the years, we endured multiple rude comments from other customers, near-misses with overturned chairs, nicked ears that caused bleeding, and hair flying in every direction. Nikki hated haircuts with a passion and she never failed to express that to everyone around her.

It was out of desperation that I came up with a solution. I began cutting her hair while she was sleeping. Before she went to bed at night, I would cover her pillow with an old sheet. Then once we got her to sleep, I would tiptoe in wearing a headlamp and proceeded to trim the hair on the side of her head that wasn't on the pillow. Then, I would wait until I heard her turn over so I could sneak back in to trim the other side, hoping, when it was all over, it would come close enough to matching the first side. After I finished, I would remove the sheet that held the hair cuttings, praying that I wouldn't wake her.

The next morning, while Nikki was focused on her breakfast, I would get behind her and cut the back of her hair and blend the sides for as long as she would allow me. She didn't like it much, but she tolerated it as long as she had food to distract her. Although her hairstyle was never a fashion statement, it wasn't all that bad. Cutting her nails required the same amount of creativity. Body maintenance was never high on Nikki's priority list.

✦ ✦ ✦

Taking Nikki to church was also a unique experience. Once, on Christmas Eve, she sat through the entire service without a peep until the final prayer, when she began giggling and clapping. I grabbed her and made a hasty retreat down the aisle, but not without receiving a few stares.

Later on, we attended a far more casual church where it was easier to handle Nikki's inconsistent behavior. Once again, Nikki surprised us with her perfect behavior. Then one Sunday during the prayer, she began making the loudest hiccupping sounds I had ever heard. Some of the younger children began to giggle, so, once again, we made a hasty exit.

One Christmas Eve, when Nikki was older, and her behavior was much more consistent, we tried taking her to church again. This time, unfortunately, she caught sight of the refreshment table as we entered and her one-track mind kept fantasizing about the big cookies she had seen on display. When I least expected it during the services, she bolted up and determinedly forced her way out of the sanctuary and toward the refreshment table in the lobby. As I attempted to hold her back, she propelled me smoothly forward as though I were on water skis.

✦ ✦ ✦

Nikki had a habit of plopping down on the ground and sitting cross-legged whenever the mood struck. We called this pose of hers a sit-down strike. Harmless enough, it would seem, but it was actually her timing and the unconventional locations she chose that were the problem. Also, whenever she decided to sit, she stayed seated. It didn't matter how hard we tried to get her up, she was fixed in place. One of her most memorable strikes occurred when we took her on a plane to visit family. Of course, she decided to sit down in the middle of the narrow aisle just as the beverage cart was coming in our direction. I tried every which way I could to get her up and back in her seat, but she wouldn't budge. From the look on the flight attendant's face, I could see she wasn't a fun-loving soul. She meant business and who could blame her? She had a job to do, and we were hindering her from doing it. Eventually, a man behind me came to my rescue and together we got Nikki up and into her seat–but not until beads of sweat were running down our faces. As thirsty as we were, and with the convenience of the beverage cart within reach, we gladly partook of the thirst-quenching offerings.

Everyone who helped us with Nikki had similar experiences to this–in restaurants, on busy streets, in parking lots, beneath heavy playground equipment, and anywhere there was room enough for her to sit down. After a while we each developed techniques to prevent these awkward situations from happening. Just when we thought we had the problem licked, Nikki would catch us off-guard. Her sit-down strikes still keep us on our toes.

✦ ✦ ✦

Since she was a baby, Nikki has gone through nonstop medical appointments of one sort or another, including: doctor visits, lab tests, diagnostic tests, therapy…the whole gamut. Of course, all of them required waiting, which none of us liked, but for Nikki, it was particularly intolerable. As she grew older and larger, she became increasingly difficult to control. If the waiting time exceeded what Nikki thought was reasonable (in most cases, no more than a few nanoseconds), she would begin acting up. Once she got the momentum going, there was very little I could do to control her. One time in a doctor's waiting room, she pulled out all the fake plants from a flower box in less than a minute. After that incident, the office staff thought it best to let us wait for the doctor in a more private room. It wasn't long before that same survival technique caught on with most of her other doctors.

On one occasion, the office window blinds became her helpless victim. It wasn't pretty, but, in the end, the room had a much better view. Then there was the chair. You know those big, heavy, barber-type chairs that are practically immovable? Well, we discovered that is not necessarily the case. Nikki once came so close to tipping one over that before the doctor came in to see her, we were forced to make one of our frequent abrupt exits.

Usually, while waiting in the doctor's office, Nikki would try to bolt out the door. I would block it the best I could and try to distract her. Brian and I had plenty of time to get creative during these waits. I think we actually came up with over fifty fun things that can be made with latex gloves. Nikki's favorite was always the rooster, but we enjoyed a few clever ones of our own.

Whenever she was ready to leave, Nikki would pick up my purse, pull out my keys, and hand them to me. She would give me her trademark stern look, and I could practically hear her thinking, "What don't you get? I want out of here."

When that didn't work for her, she became exasperated. She would put on her backpack all cockeyed and stand by the door pulling at the knob. All I could do was to sign to her: "Wait", a sign we knew all too well!

✦ ✦ ✦

With Nikki so susceptible to respiratory infections, I frequently had to keep her home to avoid catching anything contagious. That meant I would have to stay home from work and consult from there, whenever necessary. Luckily, my boss was very understanding. One day, when working at home, I was expecting an important call from a travel writer. Seconds before the phone rang, Nikki went into a full-blown seizure. Since timing is everything, I had to improvise. As I held her, monitoring the intensity and duration of the seizure, I asked Brian to answer the phone for me. I heard his innocent voice from across the room,

"My mommy will be right with you. My sister is just having a seizure."

✦ ✦ ✦

Each weekday morning, there was the usual chaos of getting both kids ready for school, while Steve and I got ready for work. One day, I wore a nice black dress, nylons, and heels, as I had an important business meeting to attend. When I entered the meeting room, one of my coworkers whispered to me, as I walked past her, "Nice butt!"

That was not something I was used to hearing, especially since I have never been known for having a shapely derriere. As I wondered what was up, I turned around and saw her snickering and pointing to my backside. I tried looking over my shoulder, but that didn't divulge any clues. Becoming more proactive, I twisted my dress around, and got a good look at the focus of conversation. It was a perfect small handprint made from Nikki's oatmeal.

"Holy handprint!" I said, as others turned to look at me.

That incident helped to break the ice and added some comic relief to the meeting.

✦ ✦ ✦

One of Nikki's favorite textures was the smooth feel of butter squishing between her fingers. After we learned, on many occasions, that this could become an issue, we tried to keep the butter out of her reach. One evening she reminded us just how smart she really was when strongly motivated. A friend of ours was coming over, someone Nikki had never met. He had a brand-new crew cut, a texture that seemed to intrigue her. During dinner she went over to rub his head. Everyone thought her behavior was cute until she dove for the cube of butter resting innocently in the dish next to our guest's dinner plate—her true objective.

There was a similar occurrence at Thanksgiving dinner. Another friend was sitting at the opposite end of the table from Steve when it appeared that Nikki had decided to get up and give him a big hug.

"How cute is that?" we all responded.

Wrong again! Nikki's arm jutted out, not for a hug but to attack the butter before we could assess what was happening. These two episodes were a small sampling of Nikki's attraction to the feel of butter whenever it appeared on the scene. We finally decided that having butter with dinner was over-rated and we stopped putting the tempting delicacy on the table.

✦ ✦ ✦

Nikki has always adored Brian and loves to spend time with him. Luckily, the feeling is mutual. At every stage of their lives, from babyhood on up, they have always found ways to have fun together. Just like with any younger sibling, he would join her in tickle-fests and roughhouse sessions, and when they were rougher than I thought reasonable, she invariably came out of the situation giggling hysterically. You can't fight that—you can only be grateful. Sometimes Nikki would even get the upper hand with Brian. Those were the times she would strategically grab for extra-sensitive body parts. Again, smart like a fox. Pardon my warped sense of humor, but I got a kick out

of watching their roughhousing and would grade their moves as if scoring an Olympic event.

"Nikki didn't learn her strategies from me," I would tell Brian, chuckling, never sure he believed me.

❖ ❖ ❖

At a somewhat calmer point in our lives, Steve and I decided we might finally be able to go on vacation, just the two of us. As we were firming up our plans, Nikki began experiencing a different type of seizure. I called her new neurologist to give him the update and I mentioned the apparently doomed trip I had been planning.

He was quiet for a while, and then he said, "This is my prescription for you: Take two piña coladas and call me from Hawaii."

"Are you sure it would be okay...?"

"Mrs. Gould. A vacation with your husband would be the best medicine for everyone—Nikki, included. She needs you to be rested and alert for whatever challenges lie ahead. I'll take care of her if she needs it, and you take care of you."

"Doctor, you've got a deal," I said, and finished making trip preparations with a new bounce to my step. My mom and dad were all lined up to come down and care for the kids and they were happy for us.

It took me about four days away from home and Steve's constant reminder to go back to sleep before I could stop waking up bright and early to administer medications. That was how programmed I was to begin each day with the kids' usual morning routine.

I will always be grateful for the prescription that Steve and I so badly needed from a sensitive doctor who understood our situation.

NIKKI'S UNIQUE ADVENTURES

I was visiting with our neighbor across the backyard fence and Nikki was happily flicking away in her sandbox right next to me. While we were talking, I saw Nikki go inside and curl up in her sun nest in our room. The sun was beaming through the window, a condition that was guaranteed to put her into a deep sleep.

After a few minutes, I entered the bedroom and saw that Nikki wasn't there, so I went down the hall to look for her. I knew all the doors were locked so I assumed she would be sitting on the couch in the living room. As I walked toward the front of the house, I heard a scream coming from outside. The front door was wide open. That's not possible, I thought. When I got to the door, I saw our neighbor pointing down the cul-de-sac and yelling, "Nikki is down the street."

When I didn't see her, I began running. My legs felt like overcooked noodles. Fear struck my body like a lightning storm. Had a car hit her? I looked up and down the street and still didn't see her. Had someone taken her? Horrific thoughts were running through my mind. As I stood there, dumbfounded, I heard a familiar sound: the jiggling of a doorknob. I moved toward it and saw movement through the fiberglass-covered entryway to the house on the corner. There was Nikki, jiggling the doorknob of our neighbor's house—a place she had never been before. So, that was it? She was out happily exploring the neighborhood and I was an emotional wreck. What I could not figure out was how she had unlocked our front door, gotten down the steep driveway by herself, and why she had targeted that particular house. These were all firsts for her, and she would never be able to tell me what had been going through her mind when she did whatever it was she was doing. To make sure this sort of adventure would never happen again, we built a fence around our front porch with a padlocked gate, and installed a second deadbolt higher up on the front door, where Nikki could never reach. The measures we take to keep our children safe!

✦ ✦ ✦

Once, when the men in our family informed us they were going on the hunting trip of a lifetime, my mom and I decided it would be a great time to take the kids on a special trip to Disneyland. After the men left on their excursion, we began our own adventure. We planned each detail of the trip carefully, preparing for anything and everything that could possibly go wrong. The drive south went smoothly and, when we arrived at our destination, we were raring to go.

It was a beautiful day and we wanted to do as much as the hours would allow. Of course, we had no way of knowing how Nikki would react to the rides. As it turned out, she proved to have the same dare-devilish streak in her that Brian and I have—meaning the faster the better. We had a full day of excitement. I loved seeing my kids having so much fun.

After dinner, my mom and I were hoping to get the kids off to slumber-land early so we could all get a good night's sleep. Nikki was soon out

like a light in the queen-size bed I was sharing with her. What a relief and a blessing. I had been hoping a full day of fresh air would help her sleep through the night, and it seemed I was about to get my wish.

All tucked in, relaxed and content after such a wonderful day, I fell asleep quickly. Out of a deep sleep, I woke up to the sound of a muffled squeal. Was I dreaming? I looked at the clock. It was 4 a.m. I felt for the presence of Nikki, who had been asleep right next to me. She wasn't there. In a confused state, I fumbled to turn on the light, which woke my mom. In tandem, we followed the squeals and found our Nikki on the floor, wedged between the bed and the wall. She was awake and content, but she was not going anywhere. For some reason, unknown to any of us, she always seemed to gravitate to snug places. And here she was again, squeezed into a space so tight that she was unable to squeeze out. I thought if I pushed hard enough I could move the bed away from the wall, but then I saw that the frame was bolted to the floor. Of course it was. Otherwise, the solution would have come too easily. So, the only option was to call the front desk and have someone come and unbolt the bed frame from the floor. Although it was an unusual request, especially at this hour, they sent someone right away. After Nikki was released from her temporary imprisonment, she got back up on the bed and started clapping. Obviously, she mistook what had happened for an amusement ride—maybe something similar to a wild adventure in Disneyland. I wasn't clapping, nor was my mom. Brian somehow managed to sleep through the entire event. Later in the morning, Brian and Nikki woke up as though nothing unusual had happened, and they were ready for another day of fun. My mom and I were a little tired, but Brian reminded us; "No time to rest guys!"

✦ ✦ ✦

Every summer, Brian spent a week with my mom and dad at their home in Oregon. This year would be the first time that Nikki was stable enough to be included. This meant I would actually have a week off, a rare and exciting prospect. Taking care of Nikki was more than a one-person challenge. Did my mom know what she was getting herself into? She assured me that she had recruited my sister and dad to help her and that everything would be just fine.

I packed summer clothes for the kids and loaded up the van. Then I drove north while my mom and sister drove south to meet us at a halfway point, where I would hand off my precious cargo. After we arrived and checked in at the motel, we spent most of the afternoon frolicking in the refreshing waters of the swimming pool. I played Marco Polo with Brian, and Nikki had fun flicking the water. Everybody was happy. Our plan was to have a nice dinner and a relaxing evening visit. After a good night's sleep, we would go our separate ways.

As the afternoon turned into evening, and the sunshine departed the pool area, we decided to get cleaned up for dinner. Since the motel room had only one bathroom, we would have to take turns using it. When Brian won the coin toss, Nikki followed behind him toward the bathroom, with none of us noticing. But as soon as he shut the door, Nikki began screaming frantically. She had gotten her finger stuck between the door and the doorjamb. As soon as Brian heard her, he opened the door, which automatically released her finger. Nikki fell to the ground, her hand shaking violently. Once he realized what was going on, Brian began crying uncontrollably. Things had gone from fun to frantic in the span of a few seconds.

I picked up Nikki as she was writhing in pain. Noticing her smashed finger was black and blue and swelling fast, I immersed it in cold water and tried to console Brian at the same time. I could tell this wasn't going to take care of itself and that Nikki needed immediate medical care. At home, I had an emergency plan and knew exactly where to go for the help she needed at any time. Where would I take her around here?

With both of my little angels screaming at high decibels, I had a hard time concentrating as I scanned the phone book for an urgent care facility. Even after I found one, I had no idea how to get there—those being the days before GPS devices revolutionized our driving. We were all still in our swimsuits as we loaded the crying kids into the car and managed to get directions from the clerk at the front desk. It was an intense, nerve-racking drive, but we made it to our destination. Once I jerked the van into park, I pulled Nikki from her car seat and reached the waiting room before my mom, sister, and Brian could even unbuckle their seatbelts and follow us inside. All I had to do was show the injured finger to the receptionist and she took us directly into the doctor's office. No doubt Nikki's piercing screams helped greatly in getting us the attention we needed. As soon as the doctor came in, I poured out the story as fast as I could and he summed up the problem just as quickly. After heating a needle, he planned to burn a small hole through Nikki's fingernail to relieve the pressure that had built up from the swelling.

I wasn't sure how to hold her to keep her still enough during the procedure. "She's terribly squirmy when she's in pain."

"No problem, Mrs. Gould. This is not my first time dealing with a child in pain. Just step back, if you will, and we'll get this done."

While Nikki was still screaming and squirming, the doctor took hold of her hand and placed it flat on the table. Then he secured it with one of his own, and with his other, he quickly pierced her injured fingernail. We smelled something burning and then we saw a fountain of blood shoot straight up a couple of feet out of her nail. Immediately, Nikki stopped screaming. It was like someone had turned off a switch. We just stood there in silence, not entirely sure what had happened.

In his dry manner, the doctor said, "Keep her hand dry for a few weeks to prevent infection. She should be fine."

Noticing my hesitation, the doctor looked at me calmly and said, "You're good to go."

"But, what if…?"

"If there are further complications, which is unlikely, you can reach me at this number."

The doctor handed me his business card and smiled reassuringly. So much for my mom's plan to take the kids swimming every day.

And that was the

end of the latest Nikki crisis. She was quickly restored to her so-called normal self and signing for food. As usual, the rest of us were left emotionally and physically drained and she was just hungry. By the time we left urgent care, it was after 5 p.m. and Nikki's internal dinner bell was sounding an alarm. One of the rules we had learned to live by was to feed Nikki on time or to expect her to blow. And, at that point, none of us had the energy to deal with that alternative.

What we had forgotten when we hurried off to the urgent care facility, and what we now needed desperately, was Nikki's diaper bag. But, considering the loud ticking of her dinner time bomb and the fact it would take us at least half an hour to get there, going back to the motel was not an option. We would have to take our chances with the diaper situation.

There was a casual diner close by, so we all flip-flopped our way inside. As soon as we were seated, we realized that we were all hungry and that this was a good move. Around the time we were finishing dinner, came the sound I dreaded hearing–the familiar gurgling inside Nikki's wet diaper. Even though I quickly scooted Nikki out of the booth, the diaper was a little too heavy for us to make a clean escape to the restroom and we left a telltale trail behind us. Fortunately, we had just made it through the bathroom door before the diaper's tapes gave way. The entire contents splattered all over Nikki, her swimsuit, the floor, the wall, and me. It was an ugly sight. The challenge for me was to clean us both and to wipe off the floors and walls before anyone else came in. I had to get extremely creative as I had no clean diapers, wipes, or a change of clothes. Of course, people did come in before I could complete my task, but they left quickly, mumbling rudely under their breath. About half an hour later, the restroom now pristine, Nikki and I walked out of there with our heads held high. What else could we do? I was still in my swimsuit, and Nikki was wearing my cover-up, which was dragging on the ground. She looked very content, as she loved that feeling that came with being diaper-free. My job was to hold it together and keep a matter-of-fact look on my face through the ordeal of getting out of the diner. It wasn't until we got to the van, where my family was waiting, that we all started laughing hysterically. Nikki was the happiest of all.

PART THREE

✦

NIKKI: AGE 6 - 11

MOMMY MOMENTS,
Some Better Than Others

I was in my weekly midmorning advertising meeting when I was summoned out for an important phone call from Brian's second-grade teacher, who was aware of our different family circumstances. She informed me that Brian was extremely upset, and that he needed me to come and console him. It seemed that one of the class's new spelling words was "mental." Since kids will be kids, the other students had been laughing and joking about terms like "mental retards." Brian was devastated by the rude comments and couldn't stop crying.

I excused myself from the meeting and immediately advised my boss that I had a family emergency and would be gone the rest of the day. Driving to Brian's school, I tried to figure out the best way to alleviate his emotional pain. When I entered the nurse's office, he ran to me and grabbed my hand, his eyes puffy and his nose dripping. Without saying a word, he led me outside the building to the car.

After we got inside, he leaned over and gave me a long, desperate hug. We stayed that way for quite a while, until his sobs became further and further apart. Then he looked up at me and began to explain in his hiccupping voice what the kids in his class had said.

"Do they know about Nikki?" I asked.

"No. They were just being mean about all disabled people."

"Do you think that maybe they weren't really being mean, but that they just haven't had as much experience being around special needs people as you have?"

"Well, yeah," he said.

"Could it be that they just don't understand?"

He looked at me quizzically in silence, and I could see his face softening as his thought processes changed.

"What do you think?" I asked.

"Well, then, I'm the best one to teach them."

"Okay, now you're talking. How are you going to do that?"

"I'm going to give my school an assembly and teach them about Nikki and her friends. I'm going to tell them they like ice cream and all the same things we do."

"Okay. Let's go talk to your principal and see what we can do."

The principal was extremely receptive. He listened to Brian's story of what had happened that day in class and to what Brian wanted to do about it. I stayed quiet, beaming with pride. When Brian said he wanted to hold an assembly, the principal looked at me and smiled. First, he asked Brian if it would be okay to start with his classroom. He agreed that was a good plan, so we went back to discuss it with his teacher. She liked the idea, so we set a date. My little second grader was now on a mission to educate the entire school. In doing so, he was able to diffuse his anger and empower himself. What a huge life lesson that was!

We went home that day and began a notebook that Brian entitled, "Special Needs People." I drew a line down the middle of a piece of paper, and we began brainstorming on all of the likes and dislikes that we all shared. Every day until Brian gave his presentation, we added new thoughts to the book.

My mom was visiting, so she got to be a part of Brian's presentation. He went to school that day as usual, and she and I got Nikki dressed up for the occasion. She didn't usually wear a dress, but that day was special. Everything was set up for us when we arrived in Brian's classroom. There were chairs at the front of the room for Nikki, my mom, and me. We sat down as Brian positioned himself at his makeshift podium, notebook open. A hush fell over the room as he began talking. Not only was everyone listening intently, they seemed to understand exactly what he was telling them. Brian explained that Nikki's ears didn't work, so we talked to her with our hands. He asked the students to plug their own ears and then let him know if they could hear what he was saying. When none of them said they could, the condition was made more real and frustrating to them.

By this time, Nikki was getting restless from sitting in one place, which was never one of her strengths. She put her feet up on me and lay down across my mom's lap, and then she lifted her dress up over her head. Thank God for tights, I thought. As we were wrestling with her to sit up, Brian turned around to see what she was doing. Since what he saw was typical behavior for her, he turned back to the class unfazed, and taught them how to sign, "Good girl."

After Brian finished his talk, Nikki was treated like a celebrity. However, we all knew who the real celebrity was that day–her brother. In the weeks to come, Brian, Nikki, and I visited more classrooms, but with one small change to the presentation. Nikki ditched the dress in favor of pants.

✦ ✦ ✦

It wasn't very long after that when Brian approached me with a logical question. "Mommy, since there's a Mother's Day and a Father's Day, why isn't there a Brother's Day?"

"You know," I told him, "I think that's a very good question and I also think we should declare it a new holiday. You definitely deserve a special day as Nikki's brother."

We chose a date halfway through the year from Brian's birthday, put it on our calendar, and have celebrated Brother's Day with him ever since. There have been gifts, special outings, and, most important, grandparent visits. Brother's Day is our unique family holiday honoring Brian, who has made such a big difference in his sister's life. Throughout his school years, Brian set an example for his friends that made Nikki and other disabled students an integral part of their school community. That's a very special brother, indeed!

✦ ✦ ✦

One morning when Brian was almost nine, he promised to keep an eye on Nikki–to play alongside her in the backyard and let me know if he need-ed any help. He was proud that he was old enough now to help me take care of her. I had wanted to be out in the yard with them, but had some house cleaning to do, as we were having friends over for dinner that night. Since both of our bathroom windows were adjacent to the backyard, I would be able to clean inside while listening for any sign of a problem from outside. All was going well, and I could hear them giggling. I was even optimistic that I might be able to finish both bathrooms before lunch.

About five minutes had passed and I heard Brian yell, "MOM!"

My heart skipped a beat. I dropped everything and ran outside, expecting to see Nikki in some dangerous situation, but, instead, she was grinning from ear to ear. The weird part was that Brian's head was leaning awkwardly on Nikki's and he was grinning, too.

"Okay. What's going on here?" I asked.

Brian looked at me sideways and laughed. "Get it?" he asked. "I'm keeping an eye on her liked you asked me to do."

"Oh, I get it. You are cute, honey," I said, smiling both inside and out. "But, tell me, are you ready to watch her for real?"

"Yes, I am," he said with that pleased-with-himself grin plastered across his face.

I went back inside the house and resumed my chores. About ten minutes later, I heard another loud, "MOM!"

Anxiously, I ran outside.

"I'm hungry," Brian said.

"That's it? That's all you need? Okay, I'll bring you guys a snack."

I went back into the house, cut up some fruit and cheese, put it on a plate, and took it out to them. Everybody was happy and, once again, I resumed my chores.

Minutes later, there was another, "MOM!"

Frustration building, I went outside again and asked Brian loudly, "WHAT?"

"Now, I'm thirsty."

"Oh, for Pete's sake. FINE! I'll get you a drink. But from now on, please call me only if you really NEED me. I have to get the cleaning done."

I served them lemonade, which was greeted with smiles of contentment.

"Remember. Call only if you really NEED me."

"Okay, Mommy," Brian said.

I was back on task. About ten minutes went by and I was starting to feel productive. Then came another loud piercing, "MOM!"

My responding voice was equally loud, as I yelled impatiently through the window, "WHAT??!!"

Slowly, in a very sweet voice, Brian said, "I NEED to tell you that... I love you, Mommy."

Talk about switching gears fast. I could feel my facial expression morph from a scowl to a smile in seconds.

Oh, he is good! Maybe he should go into politics.

I walked outside and saw that dazzling Brian grin that I knew and loved. Whatever he had actually been planning to ask me remained a mystery, but it really didn't matter. At that point, I rationalized that a clean house was completely overrated. So I put away the cleaning supplies and took off the rest of the afternoon to play outside with my amazing kids.

❖ ❖ ❖

Nikki has always liked large pictures of people's faces. Maybe she thought *People Magazine* met her requirements, or perhaps she just liked copying me. Either way, in this situation she showed me who was boss. After working all week long, my treat for myself was a leisurely bubble bath (sound familiar?) while reading the latest copy of People. I guess I loved to live vicariously through others' lives that didn't seem quite as difficult as my own. On Saturday evenings, Steve was usually home, so that was when I could count on my weekly indulgence. One particular Saturday night as I was preparing for my evening's relaxation, I ran my bubble bath, laid out my towel, placed my magazine on the counter, and lit some candles. All set, I thought. Then I disrobed and parted the mounting cloud of bubbles with my foot, proceeding to immerse myself in what felt like a little slice of heaven. It had been an unusually stressful week, and I really needed this diversion. Fully covered in water and bubbles, I sighed, opened the shower curtain, and reached out for my magazine. Just as my fingers were inches away, Nikki bolted through the door, grabbed it and ran to leave, but not before turning around and flashing her signature mischievous grin.

"What a varmint," I said, laughing out loud.

Nikki's fun character had once again shone through. Even without my magazine, I managed to enjoy my Saturday bath, but not before locking the bathroom door.

◆ ◆ ◆

We had been invited to a birthday celebration for Steve's dad, a dinner cruise excursion on San Francisco Bay. This invitation was extra special because it included Nikki. Our first thought was how exciting, and then that little voice in the back of my head reminded me it could wind up be-

ing great, or a nightmare, or anything in between. We all decided it was worth taking a chance, and we accepted the invitation with enthusiasm. The cruise was elegant and the view, breathtaking. Nikki rose to the occasion like I had never seen before. She sat patiently at the table like a lady, drank her juice out of a crystal water goblet with no spills, and ate delicately and neatly. We were all pleasantly surprised. After dinner, there was dancing. Brian got up, took Nikki's hand and led her to the dance floor, where she semi-danced with him throughout the musical piece. I sat and watched as my mommy cup overflowed. And I wasn't the only one with happy tears; it seemed to be contagious. We finished the evening by blowing horns outside on the deck while watching the moon's reflection on the still water under the Golden Gate Bridge. It was an incredible night, and remains a beautiful memory that will shimmer in my mind whenever I see moonlight dancing on the water.

✦ ✦ ✦

While we were home one weekend doing various projects, the kids were playing in the backyard. Our enclosed backyard allowed Nikki to come and go as she pleased. Steve and I were in and out of the house, multi-tasking. Late in the afternoon we decided to take a break. As we sat down on the couch, he said to me, "You know, raising Nikki is kind of like raising Daisy."

"How can you compare our special angel with a dog, even Daisy? How crass can you be?" I gasped.

Steve looked at me with a smirk on his face. Right then, I turned around and saw Nikki walking into the living room with a big smile on her face. One of Daisy's milk bones was hanging from the corner of her mouth like a cigarette. "Never mind," I said. "Point well taken."

Right then, Brian walked in and we all began laughing and wound up in a big family hug.

I wasn't sure why Daisy came in right then. She had either wanted to be part of the family hug or she wanted her bone back.

✦ ✦ ✦

After a typical sleepless night with Nikki, I was preparing breakfasts, making lunches, measuring medications, and filling backpacks for both kids. As I was reading the paperwork sent home from Brian's school, I saw a flyer for a father-daughter dance called "Me and My Guy." It was too much. I sat down and started to cry. I cried for what should have been and would never be. I cried for our lack of a normal family, and I cried, maybe most of all, because Nikki's special needs class had not been invited.

Steve asked me what was wrong. I pushed the event flyer in front of him. He looked at it for a while, and then looked back up at me and said, "I think Nikki and I should go!"

I thought about it for a minute and my smile started to return. This would give Steve an opportunity to do something very special with Nikki. She should be able to go. All I had to do was get permission from the school. Why would they say no?

After the kids and Steve left that morning, I called the school. The secretary didn't know how to answer my question, so she transferred me to the principal. He listened to my request with a sympathetic ear. Then he told me it boiled down to the fact that Nikki was still in diapers and Steve wouldn't have a place to change her.

Here we go again. Another roadblock.

Even though mothers were not allowed at the dance, I asked if I could go and just blend into the background unless needed. He finally agreed, and Steve and Nikki had a date. We were all thrilled.

I took Nikki shopping for a new dress—not even close to a favorite activity of hers. We found a beautiful, navy blue velvet dress in mid-calf length, since she usually pulled her shorter dresses up over her head. This one was perfect, made more so by the tights and hair clips we bought to match. New shoes were out, as she needed to wear her heavy-duty orthopedic boots. Who would notice them, anyway, under that beautiful dress? The big night came and we were very excited about Nikki's first date. Steve dressed up in his finest suit. I dressed Nikki to the nines and added a hint of blush and lip gloss. Steve and Nikki went through the decorated front door of the school gym with lots of hoopla and, as agreed, I entered through the back door un-

announced–being the renegade mom and all. Everyone was dressed for the occasion and enjoying their big night out while I stayed behind the scenes, video camera in hand. When Steve took Nikki out on the dance floor, he did his best to hold her interest. But she couldn't figure out what they were doing there. What she tried to do instead was turn him around so she could get up on his back for a piggyback ride. She loved her piggyback rides–and it made no difference where or how she got them.

Then, with her eagle eye she spotted a tempting cupcake on the table closest to them. From my perch, I saw what was coming next, but was too far away to intervene. With the quick, smooth moves of a seasoned athlete, Nikki dove at the table, grabbed for the cupcake, and inhaled it in two bites. Steve didn't even realize she had left the dance floor. By the time he got to her, Nikki had frosting smeared across her face, barely covering her mischievous grin. I got it all on camera and was laughing until I noticed the little girl whose cupcake she had eaten.

The little girl started wailing, "Where's my cupcake?"

Uh-oh! I climbed down from my perch, went over to get another cupcake for the distraught child, and apologized on behalf of my daughter.

Once again, Steve attempted to dance with Nikki, but she was far more interested in the dessert table. That's our girl, I thought. It was a short, but fun evening and a healthy attempt at trying to be normal.

✦ ✦ ✦

We were on our way to spend Christmas with my family. Steve had packed all of our "absolute necessities"–which were many–into the van very precisely, using every square inch of space. Then I remembered that the large Santa's bag full of Christmas gifts to take with us was still in the house. When I sheepishly brought it out to the van, I knew the response I would get from Steve, which was his trademark pinched lip, saber-sharp stare. I smiled hesitantly in response, then shrugged my shoulders and retreated quickly to the safety of the living room while a few expletives followed me inside.

As soon as I had mustered enough nerve to go outside again and see

how Steve was doing, I found festive holiday boxes stuffed in every nook and cranny of the van: on and under the seats, up along the sides, and even stuck inside a few pairs of boots.

Oh, good…it looks like we have it all.

Without a word from Steve, we all got in the car and were on our way.

I recognized a few boxes that I had recently wrapped for Nikki and decided to open one of them early to keep her entertained along the way. It was one of her favorite things, a mirror. Not just any mirror, it was a flashing, singing "Barbie" mirror, with all the requisite bling. I knew she would love it, and she did. It didn't take her long to figure out how to push the button that began the light show and started Barbie singing confidence-boosting messages, like, "You go girl…you are so beautiful…" It took less than an hour for Steve and Brian to express how completely fed up they were with Barbie's whiny voice. I was just happy that Nikki was entertained and proud that she had figured out how to use the controls, even though she replayed it to the point of exasperation.

We stopped for our normal routine. I took Nikki into the restroom while Steve and Brian filled the van with gas and washed the windshield. When Nikki and I came back, we got resituated in the van while the guys went to use the restroom and bought some snacks. As soon as Nikki was situated, she reached for her mirror and pushed the button.

Huh? Nothing but lights and no sound. That's weird.

I tried it a couple of times without any luck. If the batteries were already dead, why were the lights still working? Just then my light bulb switched on. Steve and Brian, the rascals, must have unhooked the wires in the back of the mirror, thinking they were cleverly outwitting me. But what they hadn't realized was that, anticipating how much Nikki would love this mirror, I had bought her two of them. Before the guys could get back to the van, I had found the box with the second mirror, unwrapped it, and gave it to Nikki. Instantly, her singing light show started again and she commenced clapping her delight. Even though she couldn't hear it, she liked the vibrations. It was apparent that Steve and Brian had underestimated me. I couldn't wait to see the looks on their faces when they got back in the van and saw how I had outwitted them. For the time being, I would smile on the inside and keep a straight face on the outside.

Steve and Brian were looking quite smug when they got in and hooked up their seat belts. Just as Steve was backing out of the parking lot, Nikki pushed the magical button starting Barbie's performance. Dead silence for a few seconds and then… "You go girl… you are so beautiful…"

Their reaction was everything I could have hoped for. Steve slammed on the brakes and swung his head around so fast I wasn't sure it was going to stop. Brian wore a befuddled look on his face. The two troublemakers looked at each other in disbelief. I, on the other hand, was laughing hysterically on the inside.

"Boy, that Barbie sure loves to sing," I said, innocently.

I was able to hold out for no more than an hour before I had to confess how I had bamboozled them. It was sheer poetry.

✦ ✦ ✦

Brian, Steve, and I loved to ride bikes, so I tried to find a way to include Nikki on our excursions. I looked online and found an agency in Oregon that sold custom-made bike trailers for special-needs children. *Bingo!* I thought, at first. Then I took note of the cost and wasn't sure we could swing that. So, instead, I decided to talk with Doug Brown about programs or grants that helped purchase equipment to benefit the quality of life for special needs children. He told me that he had helped start a fund for that purpose, and that I would just have to apply. Luckily, my application was approved and I was able to order a special bike trailer that would accommodate the extra weight and height for a girl as big as Nikki. It arrived about six weeks later and Brian was particularly excited that the whole family could go biking together. We planned our maiden voyage through the back roads of Pebble Beach. The weather cooperated, and the sun was out when we got ready to leave, taking a picnic along with us. Steve had hooked up Nikki's fancy trailer behind his mountain bike, since it had the widest tires.

"Put on your sunscreen, everyone, and buckle up your helmets," I announced as I put Nikki in her harness and added a baseball cap to shade her eyes, which are extra sensitive. Then, off we went with high expectations. After about fifteen minutes, Nikki began squirming and shifting her weight back and forth in her trailer, causing it to tug relentlessly on Steve's bike. He struggled to maintain control and pretend he was having fun. Nikki kept taking off her baseball cap and throwing it out of the trailer and Brian was getting tired of stopping to pick it up.

"Let's at least get out to the beach so we can have our picnic," I said.

Everyone agreed to put on a happy face and hope for the best, but as we reached the beach, the fog began rolling in and our optimism went missing in the mist.

Really? Can't just one thing go right for a change?

Even though it was cold, we hunkered down and had our picnic. On the way home, Steve's tire popped and he ended up walking his bike while pulling Nikki behind him. He was tired and frustrated and refused any help. All he wanted, he said, was just to get home. I couldn't blame him for adding a few expletives under his breath to relieve the tension. Later on, we tried to save the day with hot chocolate and cookies in front of a roaring fire. Nice try, but nowhere near resembling an equal tradeoff.

Since I was too stubborn to give up, we attempted a few more bike rides, all of those without Steve, who had already had his fill. I even special-ordered a sun canopy for Nikki's trailer to shield her from the glaring sun. It would be nice to tell you that my persistence paid off, but Nikki never really enjoyed biking as much as Brian and I did. And so ended Nikki's brief adventures in biking. We ended up donating her bike trailer to another special family, and I am hoping they got more use out of it than we did.

✦ ✦ ✦

It was Memorial Day and the kids were out of school. Since the weather wasn't cooperating with our plans for a day at the beach, and Steve had been called into work, Brian and I decided to switch gears. We wanted do something fun and special, but what?

After discussing our options for something we could do with Nikki, we decided to go out for a nice Chinese dinner. Since food was Nikki's favorite thing, and she especially loved rice, we knew she would be all for it. It usually didn't take long to be served at the Chinese restaurant, which was another plus. Upon our arrival, we were seated in a semicircular booth. That was perfect, as Brian and I were able to bookend Nikki so she couldn't get out and get into any mischief. Within minutes, the menus came. We looked them over and decided to order family style, each of us ordering one of our favorite dishes. We kept Nikki entertained until the food came by plying her with crackers, one at a time.

It wasn't long before we were served a steaming dish of sweet and sour pork, cashew chicken, and fried rice. It looked good and it smelled even better. Nikki instantly smiled and started clapping her approval. Hungry as he was, Brian began serving himself as I dished up Nikki's food. She was wearing her bib and held tight to the spoon in hand. I didn't even have the plate completely in front of her before she started scooping rice in the direction of her mouth. Okay, so the first spoonful detoured onto her lap. She would do better on the next try. As she scooped another spoonful of rice with one hand, she chose to use the other to flick rice right out of the bowl. Unfortunately, Brian's face just happened to be at the receiving end of the spray. We chuckled it off, as Brian pulled each kernel of rice out of his hair. After he cleaned up and Nikki was back on task, I tried to dish up my own food. That was a big mistake. It gave her the short opening she needed to reach out her hand and plant it right in the middle of the sweet and sour pork. It must have felt so good and slimy between her fingers that she pulled her arm back and started to clap her hands while the sticky orange sauce dribbled down her arms. The rice that had so recently occupied her plate somehow magically glued itself to her arms. Right then, she seemed to want to thank me for the exciting time she was having, so she leaned toward me with her arms outstretched for a big hug. That resulted in the transfer of some of the sticky orange goop onto me, along with a generous portion of rice.

Brian looked at me and said, "This isn't funny anymore. That guy in the black cowboy hat over there keeps glaring at us and he doesn't think it's funny, either."

I said, "How about just ignoring that man and enjoying the rest of your dinner"

But the rest of the dinner failed to get any prettier. By the time we were done eating, our table looked like the aftermath of an explosion at a rice factory. There was no way I could leave it in its present condition, so I decided on a plan.

"Brian, I want you to take Nikki to that waiting area over there, just inside the entrance. Wait for me while I clean up this mess. Okay?"

"Sure," he said. "But, hurry, Mom, the cowboy is still staring at us and I want to get out of here as fast as possible."

"Honey, no faster than I do."

As I started to wipe down the table, Brian began leading Nikki out of the main dining room. When I glanced up to check on them, I saw that the table they were passing had just been served a large bowl of rice.

Oh, no!

But before I could open my mouth to warn Brian, Nikki had already honed in on the bowl of rice like a laser beam. With her lightning fast movements and accurate aim, she reached out and flicked the rice all over the shocked young couple at the table. This would be a date neither of them would easily forget.

On the spot, Brian lost his patience. He blurted out to no one in particular, "That's it. I'm out of here."

And he walked out the door without Nikki in hand.

I stood transfixed, with helplessness written across my face, and then rushed over to grab Nikki, hoping to keep her a safe distance from the couple's table as they cleared their faces and clothes of the splattered rice.

What could I do but apologize profusely? "I'm terribly sorry. My daughter can be a bit of a handful, especially when it comes to rice, I'm afraid. May I buy you another bowl? I promise we'll be gone before it arrives."

The young man's smiling response was, "No, that's okay. I think we've had our fill of rice for today."

His lovely bride added a bit of humor. "We were married three months ago, so we're used to getting rice thrown at us."

"Not the cooked variety, though," added her groom.

As gracious as they were, my face was flushed with embarrassment.

It was a relief to get Nikki out of the restaurant and into the van with Brian, who was still mumbling under his breath. I returned to the restaurant to clean up the table as well as I could. On my way out, I left a huge tip and apologized to the staff. To this day, more than fifteen years later, Brian still refuses to enter that Chinese restaurant. His argument? The man in the black cowboy hat is probably still in there, maybe waiting for us to return.

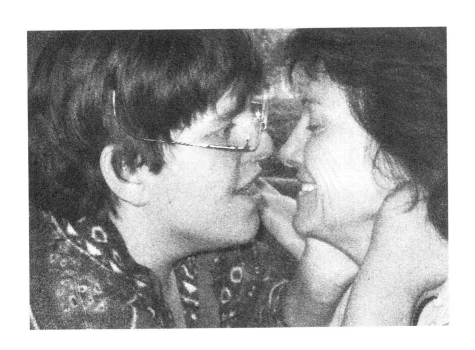

PART FOUR

✦

NIKKI: AGE 12 - 14

A LACK OF OPTIONS

Looking for a caregiver/companion for Nikki was most always a daunting task, an arduous and frustrating ordeal. It was almost as overwhelming as the tasks we needed them to perform. On a few occasions, the respondents to my ad in the local paper sounded promising. Sometimes, they turned out to be just plain weird. Do I have some juicy stories for you!

Once, I got a call from a sweet-sounding young woman. I explained what our needs were and described Nikki to her in candid terms. She was still interested, so I took out my prepared list and asked all of my routine questions. Since her answers were pretty good, I made an appointment for an interview.

She arrived on schedule, holding a large feather with beads dangling from a series of ribbons. How sweet, I thought. She brought Nikki a gift. How did she know that Nikki loved playing with feathers? However, instead of giving Nikki the feather, she began waving it back and forth over her head. Naturally frightened, Nikki jumped onto my lap. When I asked the woman what she was doing with that feather, she didn't hesitate to explain.

"This is my special healing feather. With it I will heal your daughter of all her ailments—physical and mental."

"Really?"

"Oh yes, I have healed many. I was reincarnated specifically for that purpose. But in order for the healing to work, you have to feel with absolute certainty that it will. You can't see it in my aura?"

"I looked at her in the eye and said, "No, not so much."

"It is not necessary for you to see it. Only to know that in my aura lies your daughter's destiny."

Instead of ending the interview right then and there, I let the woman continue. My mischievous side wanted to hear more. This was just too good to let go.

The woman explained that she was from Big Sur and was at one with nature. She topped it all off by telling me that, for her to accept this job, I would have to build a privacy fence in our backyard since she was totally against using indoor plumbing, including toilets. And furthermore, while in her care, Nikki would have to adhere to the same rules.

Whoa! Enough said. I pleasantly concluded the interview, showed her the way out, and I couldn't stop laughing. That night, I called everyone I knew to share my story.

Over time, I learned to watch Nikki's reactions to the applicants, as she seemed to have a sixth sense when it came to reading people. It was easy for me to tell if she liked someone. If she didn't, she would simply get up and leave the room. This time around she left within minutes after the next applicant came in the house. Not a good sign, I thought.

The woman sounded extremely desperate, and her answers were un-comfortably breathy. I was getting a strange vibe and wanted to end the interview, but I didn't know how to do it without seeming rude. That was when the answer came wafting down the hallway–a strong, pungent odor coming from the direction of Nikki's bedroom. Her timing could not have been better. I could now justify ending the interview to attend to Nikki's needs. I explained the urgency of the situation, walked the applicant to the door, and closed it behind her.

Then I ran down the hall to Nikki's room. She was sitting on her bed, covered head to toe in stinky unpleasantness, but with a victorious grin pasted across her face. I couldn't help but grin also, as I got down to the less funny business of cleaning her up. After putting her in the bathtub, I headed out to the trash container with the intention of dumping the mess. But, it wasn't that easy.

Covered in poop, I was halfway down the hall when I came face to face with the woman I had just ushered out the front door. I was shocked to find her back in my house. She pleaded with me to give her the job. I told her that I was very busy attending to my daughter's needs, and that she would have to leave. She didn't budge. She just kept begging me to hire her. I told her I was not hiring anybody at the moment, and that she must leave immediately. Finally, she backed down the hallway, walked down the driveway, and got into her car. I took out the trash, ran back into the house, and locked the door, but she sat in her car staring at the house for more than half an hour. I called Steve to let him know that we had a strange woman parked outside our house, and I asked him to stay close to the phone in case we needed help. After what seemed like an eternity, the applicant drove off. In Nikki's own way, she had made it perfectly clear that she did not like this woman, and—from what I could see—she was right once again. Pooh-pooh happens, and in this case, it was a good thing.

The next woman who called about the job told me that she had an undercover name. She liked to be called Wildfire. A quick bye-bye to Wildfire, and thanks, but no thanks.

A week later, a woman called, saying she had experience working with autistic children and elderly adults. She sounded promising. We set a time for her to come to the house, and she arrived promptly. The interview began with her describing her experiences working with the disabled. She went on to tell me that she had also been a comedienne in Las Vegas. Before I could react in any way, she looked me straight in the eye and, with a devilish grin, said, "They call me Wildfire!"

She chuckled as she saw all the color drain from my face.

Danger! Danger! My eyes opened wider and my heart started to race.

Interview over. Get out of my house!

After that, I took a break from advertising for a while. It took me time to get up the courage to try it again, but I knew I still needed to find help.

When I did finally advertise again, a woman called and offered to do the job for whatever I wanted to pay her. Numb to the whole process, I was hesitant and yet intrigued. She told me she could work for us if it was totally under the table, and she didn't have to give me her name or social security number.

"Why?" I asked.

She told me she and her brother were on the run, because he was suspected of murder in another state.

And yet another qualified candidate crosses my path.

Never again did I advertise in our county-wide newspaper. I decided to stick with small, local publications or word-of-mouth recommendations.

MAKING IT HAPPEN

One sunny day when I was leaving for work, I looked back at the house and saw Nikki's face peeking out through the living room window. She was sitting in her usual spot on the couch. This was the same scene I saw day after day. I sat there for a minute sadly watching her as warm tears trickled down my face.

It was summer and the kids were out of school. Brian was busy every day with fun summer activities: going to play at friends' houses, enjoying beach days, and sporting activities. He had many options. Nikki did not. This made him as sad as it made me. I made it my priority to research every possibility for organized activities for children with disabilities and found only one day camp in our area. Well, one is better than nothing, I thought. Excitedly, I called them, only to find out they could not take children in diapers.

"Shouldn't a day camp for disabled children be set up for all children with disabilities?" I asked.

The answer was, "No. We are not equipped for everyone."

Was this discrimination or just poor planning? There Nikki sat on the couch for yet another day, looking longingly outside for a life of sunshine and activity.

I found a teenager who offered to watch Nikki for me but she had no transportation. This meant I had to make a twenty-minute drive to pick up Nikki's new helper and a twenty-minute drive back to the house, all before heading off to work each day. And again, at the end of the workday, it required another twenty minutes to take the teenager home and a twenty-minute drive back home before we could begin our evening activities. Even with her help, Nikki's world had narrowed to the four walls of our house and our fenced-in backyard. Her basic physical needs were being met, but that was all.

I couldn't take it anymore. It wasn't fair, and it was going to change.

Brian and I decided to do something about it.

Again I made an appointment with Doug Brown, our local Special Ed coordinator. He was the person I thought was most likely to be in a position to help us–and who would want to help. While I explained that I was unable to find any summer programs for Nikki, he listened with genuine sensitivity, and nodded his head as though he understood my dilemma.

"Your problem is not exclusive to your case, Jeanie. I was recently talking to another mom who is going through the same thing."

"And what has she come up with for a solution?"

"Nothing yet, but I promise I will do my best to find one for you...for both of you."

"Doug, I can't tell you how much I appreciate that."

"Don't thank me yet. New programs don't happen overnight. You will have to be patient."

"Patience is not one of my strong suits. But, pretty much out of necessity, I am getting better at it."

I wanted to hug Doug for reigniting my hopes. "Mind if I call the other mother you mentioned?"

"Not at all. And I am sure she would be pleased to know she has an ally like you."

Doug gave me the name and phone number of the other mom, and I left his office feeling lighter than I had in months. I was sure that we could get a committee together and come up with a plan. I called the other mother that evening, and we forged an immediate bond. Just knowing that someone understood what I was going through was a huge relief. She told me she knew another family that was struggling, like we were, to find a structured program for their special-needs child. These connections soon blossomed into a planning committee of three desperate moms, Doug Brown, and of course, Brian.

It took about two years to reach our lofty goal. We had gotten the combined support of our school district, our recreation department, and our regional center, which was no easy feat. Soon, the day came when we were picking out paint colors for the room that the school district had allocated us. And, officially, our Severely Handicapped After-School Recreation

Program (SHARP) was born. We hired an extraordinary director named Lynley and a highly competent staff that included Nichole, a high school student who had also been Nikki's caregiver. After the staff was in place, we began advertising the program. We were featured in our local newspapers and even appeared in a few TV spots. Slowly, our enrollment grew to a total of eighteen children. The program filled a desperate need in our community and, the icing on the cake was the support system it helped to create for all of our families. Brian even talked many of his middle-school friends into volunteering after school to make sure Nikki and her friends had fun in a safe environment.

The SHARP program thrived for over twelve years. All of the participants grew physically and, especially, socially. They were a group of friends who cared about each other, and they had the additional support of their closely bonded families. SHARP made a significant difference in these children's quality of life. Nikki's school teacher confided that she could tell which ones of her students were participants in the program by their improved social behavior.

Even though this amazing program helped so many kids and their families, it was not an easy task to keep it afloat financially. The required staff-to-child ratio was higher than in most after-school programs, leading to higher enrollment fees. The parents covered most of the program's expenses so it would break even; however, it seemed that did not satisfy the City. They wanted all of their programs to be a revenue source, and we, they pointed out, were coming up short.

Our committee attended city council meetings to fight for the SHARP program. We agreed to begin fundraising events to keep the program alive, and we started a scholarship fund for students whose parents could not afford the fees. These efforts got us a reprieve of about a year, during which time we were able to build a substantial scholarship fund. Eventually, due to staff changes and financial cuts to the program, the enrollment figures started to drop. Again, we worked hard to get the word out through newspaper articles and TV interviews, trying to rebuild the program. We received some donations and hobbled along until finally the City lost interest and pulled the plug.

Luckily, one of our committee members was familiar with our local chapter of a nonprofit group, one whose sole mission was to provide for the unmet needs of people with disabilities. We contacted them, attended multiple meetings, and submitted written proposals. They eventually agreed to include our program under their nonprofit umbrella.

For about a year, they maintained the existing program; then they began making changes that were not advantageous. SHARP started experiencing financial difficulties again, sparking rumors that the program would have to close. When our planning committee heard about this and questioned the non-profit agency, they explained that the program was losing money every month and that if we could not change it into a money-making program soon, it would close permanently. We were all very upset.

At the next meeting, we asked the agency to dip into the money from the $30,000 scholarship fund that we had raised to help cover the program's monthly deficit. That was when the ugly truth came out. They had absorbed our scholarship fund into their own bottom line when they brought our program into their agency and the money was no longer available to our program. Now we were all in shock. When we requested copies of SHARP's profit-and-loss statements, the management of the agency became very defensive.

Ultimately, the bottom line is always about the bottom line. It did not appear to any of us that it had anything to do with whom they were helping, or why. These agency representatives should have reread their mission statement as a reminder of their commitment.

After an unsettling period for the children and their families, the program's doors closed for good. Everything that we had worked for so passionately, for so many years, became nothing more than a vivid memory. With nowhere else to go, the kids had to go back to sitting on their couches in their limited realities. The parents were forced to leave work early or find alternate supervision for their children. The family support system that had been so carefully built and nurtured by the program slowly dissolved away.

I still get sad whenever I think about the unnecessary demise of that beautiful program, especially when I consider all of the benefits it offered to so many in need of them. At least for twelve solid years we were able to make a difference in the lives of many special-needs kids and their families. We had a good run and we will always be indebted to Doug Brown, without whom the program might never have become a reality.

✦ ✦ ✦

As each year came to a close, we had to deal with placement meetings to determine Nikki's next class assignment. The makeup of the special-needs classes was based on the students and their particular needs, so movement to different schools and classrooms was inevitable. Each transition brought new challenges.

Before each placement, I would review the classroom options. Some, I felt would be a good fit, while others made me incredibly sad, as it looked as though the children were no more than parked for most of the day, as the clock slowly ticked away toward three o'clock. I knew Nikki's options were limited due to her multiple disabilities, but I just could not let that happen to her.

The seed that was planted with the first special education class in our district bore fruit and began to grow and multiply. This inspired a welcome shift in the school district's approach, and, as a result, more classes emerged. It was a slow process, but eventually we had classes at the elementary school, at the middle school, and then eventually at the high school. Our district was slowly becoming known for creating an accepting atmosphere for special-education students. And, here again, a lot of that was due to Doug Brown, who saw and understood the needs of our families.

ON HER OWN TERMS

I got a call at work from Nikki's school, and was told that a woman driving by the school building had noticed Nikki sitting unattended on the sidewalk, right next to the road. Suspecting something was wrong, the woman parked her car and ran inside to tell the secretary. A staff member went to get Nikki and walked her back to the classroom. No one could figure out how Nikki had gotten out to the roadside on her own. She was a one-on-one student. Where was her teacher? How could this have happened?

The secretary told me not to worry, "The situation is now under control. But I am required to notify you of what happened."

"What did happen?"

"Nikki's teacher took her and another student out for a walk. The other girl fell down, and, while the teacher was tending to her, Nikki wandered off. She knew where the bus picked her up every day, so she must have decided to head there."

"I can't believe the teacher took her eye off Nikki for that long. Didn't she notice she was missing?"

"In the heat of the moment, her teacher apparently forgot about Nikki. She was so focused on taking the injured girl back to the classroom."

"And when did she finally realize it?"

It wasn't until the secretary brought Nikki back to class that she realized her mistake. Understandably, it was not long before I switched Nikki to a different classroom.

✦ ✦ ✦

We had been without after-school care for Nikki for quite a while. I had to leave work early every evening, which wasn't very job-friendly. Now that she was older, bigger and stronger, it was harder than ever to find a caregiver. Her size and the fact that her hormones were announcing themselves loudly and frequently did not make for a compatible combination. Desperate to find someone, and because my options were limited, I placed another ad in a local paper, even though my experience with such ads had brought me only bizarre results. I was temporarily encouraged when the calls starting coming in, but once I began explaining the details of the care Nikki needed, the callers would hurry to end the conversation.

One night while I was cooking dinner, I got a call from a young woman named Wendy who was interested in the position. Here we go again, I thought. I began my canned speech about our situation and Nikki's needs, expecting the usual response. I was shocked when she said, "She sounds like a miracle child."

Had I heard her right? After I collected myself, putting dinner on hold, I said, "That's exactly what she is—a miracle child."

I could not believe what I was hearing. My pessimistic side reared its ugly head and reminded me: if it sounds too good to be true, it probably is. But, I wanted to know more. We continued our conversation and began to compare notes about our lives. When I mentioned Nikki's disease, she said, "Yes, I know it all too well. My daughter, who is Nikki s age, was diagnosed with the same disease when she was very young."

"Really! How is she doing now?"

"She's actually doing well. Hers, thankfully, was a much milder case than Nikki's. She outgrew most of her symptoms by the time she was seven. I feel blessed."

"I can imagine. Do you have any other children?"

"My other daughter is two years older. She's healthy, however, she has to deal with dyslexia."

"No way! My son has dyslexia, too."

In the course of this conversation, we marveled over the amazing coincidences we shared in our children. We both had daughters with the same disease, both of whom had siblings two years older who had been diagnosed with dyslexia at the same age.

Okay, this is just too weird.

We went on to talk about our husbands, who, remarkably, also shared similarities. They each worked as computer techs, were Eagle Scouts, and were currently volunteers in their local Boy Scouts chapters.

Wendy said she had been home schooling her two daughters through their grade-school years. Now that they were approaching high-school age, she and her husband, Darren, had been discussing the possibility of her looking for a part-time position. "I'm looking for something in the evenings to help cover some of the extra expenses coming our way."

"How did you find my ad?"

"I was taking care of a sick friend this morning when I noticed the local paper sitting on the edge of her bed. For the first time in ten years, I decided to look through the classifieds. Your ad was the first thing I saw."

"I guess you know better than most the challenges involved."

"I do. But I knew immediately it was what I wanted to do. Our conversation only confirms my initial instincts."

"I feel the same. There is too much common ground here. It's got to be more than coincidence." I truly felt we had some sort of connection.

Excited at the prospect of meeting each other in person, we scheduled a meeting for the following evening. I tried not to let my hopes get too high. That next evening, I was hoping to get Nikki fed and bathed before Wendy arrived. We were just finishing up when the doorbell rang. As I opened the door, Nikki made a beeline from her bedroom, pushing me aside. She grabbed Wendy's hand, led her to the living room, and pushed her down on the couch. Then she sat as close to her as she could, cupping her hands around Wendy's face to make direct eye contact. After focusing on her face for about thirty seconds, she started clapping. Uncharacteristic of Nikki, she remained glued to Wendy's side the rest of the evening. Later on, Wendy explained to me that she felt Nikki was looking into her soul, building a heart-to-heart connection.

"She must have liked what she saw from the start," I told her. "Just so you know, my daughter has an amazingly accurate sense about people."

From the moment Wendy walked in and before I even had a chance to introduce myself, Nikki finished the interview in her own way. She showed me, without hesitation, this was a GO! The most amazing part of it was that Wendy seemed unfazed by the uniqueness of the situation. She and I talked for hours like long-lost friends. As for Nikki, it was love at first sight.

Serendipity? Fate? Luck? Or was it no less than an unqualified miracle? From the day of Nikki's birth, meeting Wendy was one of the best things that happened to us as a family. This chance encounter positively changed my life, Nikki's life, Wendy's life, and the lives of everyone in both of our families. Our incredible relationship continues today, as, over the years, our families have basically blended into one.

The first time Wendy looked after Nikki, we gave her a list of things to look out for with Nikki. However, we had already learned that you never really got it until you experienced her firsthand.

Nikki was as strong physically as she was headstrong. On that initial occasion, Nikki was charging down the hall and Wendy tried to slow her down. Underestimating my daughter's strength, she grabbed the pockets of her overalls and was stunned when she ended up with two torn pockets in her hands. Nikki, on the other hand, remained unfazed, and continued on her merry path.

When it was bath time, Wendy began running the water and then turned her back for a few seconds to grab a towel. Nikki, meanwhile, had climbed into the tub of warm water with all of her clothes on, even her brand-new leather orthopedic boots. That was a first for Wendy. By the time she had

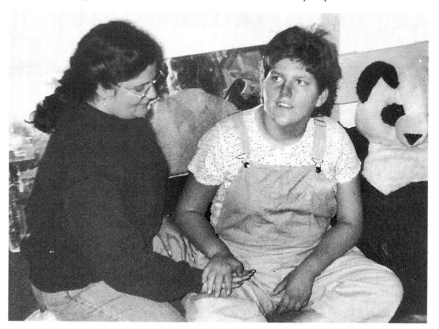

cleaned Nikki up and gotten her into her pajamas, she was worn out, and that was only after having been with her for a couple of hours. Wendy had no idea what would happen next, but she was determined to keep going. She decided that if we, as a family, were able to do this on a daily basis, so could she. She would just have to build up her Nikki stamina.

It took a while before Wendy felt comfortable taking Nikki out in the community, as she never knew what to expect—except, of course, the unexpected. Starting with short walks up and down the street, they eventually advanced to the park. Then one afternoon when she was feeling particularly brave, Wendy decided to take her to Costco to pick up a few things. She also planned for them to have lunch there. With Nikki's attention span being especially short, they didn't manage to do much shopping. While Wendy was ordering lunch, Nikki's glance was focused on a little boy next to her eating a plump, juicy hot dog. A few seconds later when Wendy turned around, she was stunned to see what had happened. In the blink of an eye, Nikki plucked the hot dog right out of its bun, and out of the boy's grasp. He looked shocked and helpless as he watched Nikki delightedly chomping down his lunch, while he sat inconsolable with his empty bun. Apologies all around, and another hot dog for the little boy.

Wendy soon learned that Nikki was not simply partial to hot dogs. On another occasion, as they were entering a fast food restaurant together, Nikki, quick as lightning again, grabbed a hamburger right out of a diner's hand. Another hamburger, please.

One of the first times Wendy experienced a sit-down strike, it was a doozy. She and Nikki were crossing a busy street when Nikki plopped herself down in the middle of the crosswalk on a four-lane road. After a while, cars started slowly going around them. Wendy tried everything, but she could not budge Nikki. It took the additional muscle of a true Samaritan bystander to get Nikki out of the street and onto the safety of the sidewalk. Another time, Nikki pushed Wendy into a men's public restroom, figuring there would be a mirror inside for her to look at herself. Wendy's strong-arm tactics proved fruitless in trying to get her out. Finally, a nice gentleman entered the room, and once he got over the shock and surprise of seeing two females in a males-only space, he offered his able assistance.

✦ ✦ ✦

Easter was just around the corner, and our beautiful spring weather was at the peak of perfection. Festivities would be extra-special this year, as it would be the first holiday in which both sets of grandparents would be sharing in their grandkids' excitement together. Brian and I had carefully orchestrated a full agenda for our special day.

First on our list was the outdoor sunrise service. We would get up really early, dress in warm clothes, and join many of our friends at a special church service overlooking the ocean. Everyone would sing and pray, while hoping to see the sunrise instead of the customary fog bank. Of course, if you were on Nikki patrol, you walked around the park the entire time instead, hoping at least to hear parts of the Easter sermon.

Our next activity would be the family Easter egg hunt in the backyard. Brian had reached the age when the community egg hunt no longer seemed cool, yet he could still have fun in the cocoon of our own backyard. Nikki couldn't have cared less about it, but she always went through the motions to humor us. She probably thought, why pick it up if you can't eat it? Or, what's up with the funny basket?

We had also planned a special Easter meal that we knew would please everyone: champagne-glazed ham, asparagus hollandaise, scalloped potatoes, spinach salad, and squiggly gelatin eggs for Nikki. We would top it off with my traditional three-layer whipping cream Easter cake. After making the grocery list and shopping for essentials, we did all the early preparation together. Following the meal we would all take a leisurely walk to the beach and enjoy the sunset. What a perfect day it would be!

The day before Easter, Steve's parents came in from San Francisco, while my parents arrived after their long drive from Oregon. Lots of hugs and kisses all around. Now that we were together, our celebration could begin.

In our small house, eight of us rising early was a recipe for chaos. Before the sunrise service, we were all competing for the bathroom at the same time. Add Nikki to the equation, and mass confusion ensued. All in all, even though we were just a little late, we did get to see the glorious sunrise, which was well worth the effort.

When we got home, Nikki plopped down on her bed to catch up on the sleep she had missed. A couple of us went out back to hide the eggs that Brian and I had colored, along with the batch that Steve's dad had lovingly colored back home and brought with him. Some eggs were hidden for the super-sleuth, Brian, and some were strategically placed in plain sight for Nikki. We woke Nikki up and all gathered for the traditional egg hunt. There was plenty of cheering, coaxing, clapping, and camera-clicking!

Afterwards, it was time for our special Easter dinner. Brian and I were going to "wow" them with our plan to serve the meal in courses, just to make it seem extra-special. We had expanded the table so that it took up the entire dining room and part of the living room, and set it with an Easter tablecloth, flowers, pastel colored napkins, and white china plates. A chocolate Easter bunny stood proud at each place setting.

The first course was a spinach salad, served with hot-cross buns. We were all at the table except for Nikki, who was, luckily for us, happily playing on her bed. This meant we could all enjoy the salad course in peace. Nikki wasn't much of a salad-lover, anyway. She was more a main course, cut-to-the-chase, kind of girl.

As I was finishing my last bite of salad, I heard an odd noise coming from Nikki's bedroom—a light splashing sound. It wasn't unusual for her to go into the bathroom and turn on the faucet so she could randomly flick water; but this sounded a little different than that. While Steve was picking up the salad plates, I decided to do a quick check on Nikki.

When I got to her bedroom, I saw that Nikki was sitting on her bed, smiling. However, she looked somewhat lower in her waterbed than usual. A few more steps toward her, and I saw the cause of her contentment. She was seated in a rectangular pool that was forming on her bed, and flicking herself silly with the warm water that was rising around her from an unknown source.

Houston, we have a problem.

I didn't want to alert the masses, so I called to Steve in a very controlled voice, "Steve, could I see you for a minute?"

The last thing I wanted to do was disrupt this special dinner that Brian and I had spent weeks planning. Even though he was in the middle of a conversation, Steve recognized the urgency in my voice. He walked down the hall and took in the scene.

Our special angel was sitting in her own private hot tub, where no hot tub was supposed to be. As I watched, Steve's facial expression changed from cordial and content to frustrated, and then to just plain angry.

That was when he turned to me and said, "Well, Happy F***ing Easter."

By now, everyone knew something was going on, so they started gravitating to the bedroom, one at a time, to satisfy their curiosity. This turn of events had never been imagined in our carefully scripted plans. Once again, we had to put our AAA (Adapt And Adjust) concept into action. Oh, how Brian hated those words and the disappointment they invariably brought.

We left our parents in charge of the rest of the dinner. While they enjoyed the meal, I got Nikki changed into dry clothes. Steve took charge of finding the leak and discovered one of Nikki's favorite hand mirrors wedged down between the waterbed mattress and frame. It had broken and then cut a hole in the waterbed.

Now, instead of enjoying our dessert course, we all ended up clearing out Nikki's room so everything could dry out. We had to dismantle the bed, pull back the carpet, blot up the water, and attempt to dry out the plasterboard before we could assess the damage. With Nikki's room stripped, she was confused and out of sorts.

It wasn't until much later, after we were all exhausted, that we were able to sit down and enjoy the last course of our so-called "perfect dinner." I was reminded again that life happens while you're planning something else.

✦ ✦ ✦

I wanted to be as involved in Brian's extra-curricular activities as I was busy with meeting all of Nikki's needs. Since I grew up playing basketball with my dad and older brother (who later was a coach), I though it would be fun to be a coach for the community's recreational basketball league. When I asked Brian what he thought about the idea, he got excited.

A similar response from the recreation department was, "Absolutely, yes. And good timing. We're seriously short on volunteer coaches this year."

"Perfect. This will be so much fun. And my son will be thrilled."

I waited for a volunteer application to come in the mail and when it arrived, I was surprised to find it addressed to Steve instead of me.

I called and expressed my confusion. "There must be some mistake. I was the one who volunteered and was accepted, not my husband."

After checking their files, the voice on the other end said, "So sorry. I must have misunderstood our previous conversation."

"How's that?"

"Well, we've never had a female coach before. We're a little concerned about how the male coaches might accept you."

By the time I finished pleading my case, it was agreed to give me "a try."

"Frankly, I'm surprised it's even an issue," I said.

What's up with that sexist attitude? Oh, well. I'm in, and that's what counts.

At our first coaches' meeting, the men seemed uncomfortable having a woman in their midst. I think one of them even felt sorry for me and tried to take me under his wing. He advised me about how their good old boy club worked. Whatever, I thought. That was their problem, not mine.

I've got a team and we're going to have fun. Let the games begin!

I was worried, though, about how I was going to manage everything, since I didn't have consistent care for Nikki during the scheduled after-school practices. Sometimes, I would need to bring her along with me and play it by ear. The team surprised me by embracing Nikki. We named our team the Braves, and I found they truly were the Braves in every sense of the word. During games, Nikki would sit at the end of the players' bench in her oversized, raspberry-pink stroller. As the coach, I had to be at the opposite end of the bench. It was arranged that when Brian wasn't playing, he would sit next to Nikki and keep her entertained. When it was his turn to enter the game, he appointed one of his teammates to take over Nikki-patrol. It became an honor among the boys to entertain Nikki because she was "cool." Eventually Nikki had her own team uniform and became the Braves' mascot. Oh, and, by the way, our team won the championship that year.

The next season, the coaching application was sent to me, not Steve. I wound up coaching the team all through Brian's middle-school years. I knew this was a time of transition for young boys, and at this point, it might not be cool for him to be hanging out with his mom and his younger sister, never mind the added issues of her being disabled. Brian continued to blow me away with his unconditional love for Nikki and his acceptance of her special needs, even at his tough age. I knew that, in Brian, I had been blessed with an incredible human being, and I have never ceased to be grateful.

✦ ✦ ✦

On your marks; get set; go! The gun went off and the Special Olympians ran toward the finish line. Nikki was on the starting line with the rest of the participants, but she was not as competitive as the others. In fact, she would rather have been sitting in the grass twirling flowers. She was a good sport, though, and humored us. We would have to lure her to the finish line with a Happy Meal, just to keep her motivated and moving forward. When, eventually, she completed the race, the patient crowd let go with a rousing cheer. She was happy too, as she could finally have her lunch.

For years, we continued to get a large group of friends and families to volunteer at the local Special Olympics event. It was always an exciting, fun, and fulfilling day for everyone involved. We would top off the occasion with a barbecue at our house, enjoying the camaraderie and sharing our individual stories from the event. Some were endearing and motivating, some

were sad and frustrating, and some were just plain funny. The support and validation that our family received each and every time was overwhelming and it gave us the motivation to do it again the following year.

✦ ✦ ✦

Nikki loved riding in the car or the school bus so much that she wanted to be riding most of the day. During the week, she was usually pretty content. She had daily bus rides to and

from school, field trips at school, and back and forth trips with me to shuttle Brian between home, school, and his many sporting activities. Weekends were a different story. After working all week, I needed to get household chores done. Nikki was not happy with my lack of free time to drive her around and she never hesitated to show me how she felt.

When Steve and I were both home on the weekends, we would take turns driving Miss Nikki. Although we had various other things we needed to accomplish, we learned that this was essential to keeping the peace. It got to the point where I seriously considered interviewing taxi drivers, to see if I could hire one to drive Nikki around just so we could get something else done.

We were thrilled when Brian got his driver's license. It was a win-win situation. He wanted to drive, and Nikki wanted to be driven. She especially loved it when she got to sit in the backseat of Brian's friend's truck, which had subwoofers under the seat. She had always been a fan of anything that vibrated, so this was a big hit.

Sometimes, we even paid the boys for participating in the Driving Miss Nikki program. However, it didn't come without a price for the teenagers. Brian once confessed with a smirk on his face, "You know, Mom, driving around with Nikki does not make me babe-magnet material."

◆ ◆ ◆

One evening, I had to leave Nikki in the bathtub for a few minutes to answer the phone, as I was waiting for an important call from her doctor. I never figured out what possessed her, but right then she got out of the bath and walked down the hall to the living room, her naked, plump body dripping with bubbles. Then she plopped down on the couch at precisely the same time Brian's buddy came out of the kitchen and into the living room. With lightning speed, his friend ran back to the kitchen and began blubbering something Brian couldn't decipher. When Brian peeked around the corner, he saw the nude Nikki, knowingly nodded his head, and smiled. After Brian walked her back to the tub, he told his friend that he'd never seen him move so fast. "If I were you, I'd visualize that image when you're out on the football field. You'll never run quicker in your life."

Brian's friend didn't find it funny, but we couldn't stop laughing.

HORMONAL HAVOC

Nikki's thirteenth year was a complete blur, and not in a good way. I realized I was not hiding the pain when I went to the pharmacy late one night to pick up Nikki's meds. The pharmacist, whom I had known and trusted for years, took one look at me and gasped, "What on earth happened to you? You look awful!"

My answer back to him was, "Well, I feel even worse, but I guess that means I'm still alive."

It was Brian's freshman year in high school. I was working full time. Nikki's behavioral outbursts had begun to escalate into out-and-out fits of rage. We had no idea what was happening or why, and I didn't know what to do. I had called every doctor we knew, and each kept referring me to yet another specialist.

I took Nikki from one specialist to the next, each time describing what we were going through. Many of them dismissed her case as too complicated and advised us to find someone else. Even the head of psychiatry at our local hospital turned us away with the same response after I had waited three months for the appointment. None of us, including our existing team of doctors, could figure out if Nikki's erratic, violent behavior was due to seizure activity, or if they were simply behavior-driven. Could her hormones be the root cause? What could we do to help her? She would scream and bang her head so hard on the wall between her bedroom and ours that the pictures on our walls fell and broke. This ritual continued, night after night.

At least three times a week, Nikki's school would call to ask me to come pick her up because of her fits. She was acting out in school, as she was at home, and her body was constantly taking a beating. Her teacher told me she would throw herself onto the pavement outside, hammering her chin down onto it until it looked like raw hamburger meat. Once, she rushed out of her class with such force, she hit a railing at her waist, flipped around, and landed on her back, smashing the back of her head onto the pavement with a loud crack. I could not expect the school to deal with these major disruptions, nor to take responsibility for her unpredictable behavior. At the same time, I needed to keep my job. It was definitely hard to keep working full time under these circumstances, but our finances and our insurance coverage needs left me no choice.

No one knew whether to treat the seizures or the behavioral outbursts, but Nikki's pediatrician hung in there with us until we had a plan. Once again, after waiting for months, we got an appointment with both the top neurologist and top psychiatrist at a prestigious hospital in the Bay Area on the same day. This was nothing short of a miracle. Considering their credentials, we thought for sure they would give us a definitive answer.

The neurologist started Nikki off with an electroencephalography (EEG) scan, to see if they could locate significant seizure activity. Holding her down while they glued seemingly hundreds of probes to her head was nearly impossible. She was squirming, screaming, twisting, and banging her head the entire time. I was in the hospital bed with her, trying to hold her down, but I was no match for her strength and sheer will to get out of there at all costs. Sweaty and exhausted from the struggle, we waited over an hour for the results. When the neurologist came in, he told me the EEG was inconclusive, but based on what he could see in the scan, her outbursts did not appear to be seizure-related. At that point, the simple conclusion should have been that if seizure activity was not the cause, behavior had to be. We were getting closer to the answer and moved on to the next appointment.

After doing more extensive workups and firing a barrage of questions at us, the psychiatrist determined that, after all, it was seizure activity, not behavior, that was definitely at the root of her outbursts. So much for the consistent diagnosis of experts.

We had been struggling with this situation for over six months now, and we still had no answers. We were not sure how much longer we could keep going on like this. Nikki's eyes looked hollow, with large dark rings etched beneath them. I ached for her and all of us. One night after I had finally gotten her to sleep, I ran out of the house and drove around for hours, bawling and belting out the song that became my new mantra: "Bring on the Rain." I was hoping either God would hear me or that I would pass out from exhaustion. I desperately needed both.

This period was also unnerving for Steve and devastating for Brian, who was hurting for Nikki, for me, and for himself because of everything he was missing out on as a new high school student. I kept telling him we were okay, and I pleaded with him to try out for a sport or hang out with his friends after school. Eventually, after Brian talked with the football coach, After some discussion with the coach, Brian decided to try out for the football team. Yet still, after practices, he would dash home to help me out with Nikki.

Not too far into his first semester, one of Brian's teachers called and asked me to meet him at the school. When I arrived at the designated room, I faced three teachers sitting around a table, who proceeded to inform me that they had noticed a huge change in Brian. He had become much more solemn, was isolating himself socially, and had taken to wearing sunglasses in class to hide his eyes. His grades were also being affected. The teachers had known about his disabled sister, but they had no idea what he was actually going through. Obviously, I had also been in the dark about how much Brian was being affecting by Nikki's behavior. When I explained the situation to the teachers, they were better able to understand. As a consequence of our meeting, Brian now had an incredible support group among his teachers at school, and we all agreed to work together to help him through this difficult time.

Once the meeting was over, I went to Brian's classroom and pulled him out of school for the day. "We're going out to lunch, and then you're taking the rest of the day off."

"I can't do that. I can't walk out of school without permission."

"You have permission. I just had a long talk with your teachers who not only excused you, but insisted on you taking the day off."

And off we drove to a nearby restaurant. Once we started talking over lunch, everything came pouring out, as though a tap had burst open.

"Why didn't you tell me how this was affecting you at school? Why didn't you feel comfortable talking to me about it? I thought we were both clear about never holding back."

"I just didn't think you could handle any more stress. I know that Nikki is more than most people could handle, and I didn't want you to have to take on anything else. I thought I could handle it myself."

As we hugged, Brian and I made a solemn pact that day to always be up-front and honest with each other about our feelings, our concerns, our struggles, and our ongoing challenges throughout the rest of our lives. We honor that agreement to this day.

✦ ✦ ✦

One night shortly after that, Nikki's rage-fits got so bad that it became necessary for me to call the emergency hotline at our local hospital. I found out that being thirteen years old put a person in a medical nowhere land. The pediatric emergency attendants could only help Nikki if she was twelve or under and the adult helpline could not help her unless she was fourteen or over. Talk about falling between the cracks. We desperately needed emergency help and we needed it immediately.

I phoned many different agencies until I finally found one that said they would try to help us. It happened to be a crisis team in San Jose that was an hour and a half away. While I was on the phone with them, I could see Nikki injuring herself and Brian doing his best to protect her. I knew it would take a long time for the crisis team to reach our house, so we had to use desperate measures to keep Nikki as safe as we could until they arrived.

The only thing we could think of to do was throw a blanket over her, with each of us holding down two of its corners with our feet and hands, cocooning her for her own safety. Otherwise, wihout restraint, she would have run directly into walls, banged her head until her nose bled, spattering the walls with her blood, as she shook her head frantically back and forth. She would climb up on the bathroom counter and bash her head into the mirror. She even banged her teeth down onto the porcelain of the bathtub, chipping her front teeth. She would lunge at me like a caged tiger that had just gotten loose, knocking me into the wall, and running past me trying to get out the door. It was as if she was trying to escape, if from no one but from herself. One thing I knew for sure; whatever was going on was more than my brain could handle.

About twenty minutes before the crisis team arrived, Nikki finally ran out of steam. By the time they showed up, she had almost passed out from exhaustion. The medics checked her thoroughly, but they did not find anything that could help us determine the cause of her behavior. It was evident from her injuries, her catatonia, and the ravaged living room that Nikki had just come down from a frenzied state.

That was what gave me the idea. The crisis team had seen that we'd been to hell and back, and they believed what we told them. What if Nikki's doctors were able to see her rage-fits? No one with a conscience would then be able to deny us help. That was it! I bought a video camera to film her fits and verify what Nikki was actually going through. The night I brought the camera home, we read the directions and figured out how to use it. We set it up on a tripod, and it was ready to go, just in time for the predictable nighttime fit. And sure enough, Nikki started banging her head, rhythmically at first; then her behavior escalated into a full-blown fit. She was bashing her head into the wall, arching her back, and kicking and screaming. The blood began to fly around the room. It took everything I had to not run to her and protect her thrashing body. We needed this on film, and we were going to get it. I had to keep reminding myself that her room was completely Nikki-proofed so she could not do any major bodily harm. All of her furniture was bolted to the walls and had rounded edges. Her windows had Plexiglas coverings screwed into the frames, to protect her from the glass. There was cushiony carpet on the floor, and there were large stuffed animals in every corner to soften her falls. Her bedroom door was a half-door, so we could see and hear her at all times and be positioned to react at a moment's notice.

With the video we shot that night, I now had proof of her alarming behavior. Confident the video would make our case, I kept pushing the system until I was granted an appointment with the head of psychiatry at a large nearby hospital. I told the doctor that I had recorded the behavior he needed to see, and that was what finally got us in the door.

Nikki and I drove to the doctor's office, video in hand. I described to him the crisis we had been living through for almost a year, and told him how desperately we needed his help. He provided the equipment I needed to play the video, which I made him watch for at least ten minutes. He final-ly raised his hands and said, "Enough! I will try to help you. Just understand that this will be no more than a crapshoot."

"That's fine with us. We have nothing to lose," I told him.

The doctor's words were the most beautiful I had heard in years, and I ran around the table and hugged him. Judging from the look on his face, he was not expecting me to do that. Of course, he had only the slightest concept of what he had just signed up for.

He was right. The journey was a crapshoot—a long, exhaustive process of trial and error, involving many different psychotropic medications and combinations. They were potent medications with volumes of side effects, but we had no other options. There were many appointments; there was regular monitoring of Nikki's blood levels; there were ups and downs, er-ratic behavior and setbacks; but, through it all, this doctor stuck with us. It took months of trial and error to find a combination of medications that was effective in calming her down, but he did it. We were finally able to take a long and well-deserved deep breath.

Hallelujah!

Only a few weeks later, the pharmacist called me with bad news. He told me that one of the new medications that Nikki had been taking was being pulled from the market immediately, due to low sales volume.

"It's all about the bottom line," the pharmacist said.

"That can't be. They can't just stop producing this medication. What about all the people who depend on it for their treatment? They have to be taken off slowly. This isn't a simple aspirin product; it's a heavy-duty, mind-altering drug."

Exasperated, I left work and drove to the pharmacy, whose staff, by now, was like my second family. They were as upset as I was, but there was nothing they could do. The medication would no longer be available, and they were already completely sold out. They agreed there would be major health consequences for Nikki if I could not find enough of it somewhere to taper her off slowly. Back home, I worked my way through the entire phonebook listing for pharmacies, even calling those in surrounding towns. Mostly, I got the same story; this wasn't a popular drug with doctors as it was so heavy-duty and pharmacies only special-ordered it by request. After making calls for over an hour, I found one pharmacy that had eighty pills left. Those pills would be just enough to give Nikki the usual two-week tapering-off period. I didn't even ask the price. I just jumped in the car and prayed I would get there before they closed. Fortunately, I made it there with ten minutes to spare and they had the prescription ready for me when I walked through the door. They told me that since this medication had already been pulled from the market, my insurance would not cover it.

"It's not like I have an option," I said.

When the pharmacist handed me the bill, however, all I could say was, "Yikes! No vacation again this year."

Her doctor continued to look for another medication. It took a while, but he found a drug that had just been approved, and he suggested we try it. Again, we had nothing to lose, and, again, it would be a crapshoot. At that point, my whole life felt like a crapshoot. Fortunately, our luck held out. Within weeks, Nikki had easily transitioned onto this new medication and was back to being her old, happy-go-lucky self. Oh, how we had we missed our Nikki!

Brian has told me repeatedly that he doesn't remember that year. Maybe it's for the best.

♦ ♦ ♦

Nikki

We call her Nikki; they said she would be slow; still,
she has taught us more than we could ever know.

From laughter to tears, our feelings flow;
our emotions range from high to low.

Many are happy and many are sad,
sometimes upset and sometimes glad.

When she is happy, we feel dear; when she is mad, we feel fear.
Mixed feelings of love and fear carry on from year to year.

Even though I love her so, I sometimes feel that she must go.
It hurts me to think that my feelings are true,
but sometimes I don't know what else to do.

I love her dearly, I want you to know;
and I get fed up, this is also so.

I do my best to give it my all, yet I'm also afraid that I will fall.
Living with all these emotions
has created the foundation to my devotion.

Nikki has allowed me to see how to be me.

Brian Gould (age 15)

✦ ✦ ✦

Even early on, the well-meaning professionals from our regional center, the people assigned to Nikki's case, kept suggesting that we seriously consider putting her on a waiting list for a group home, one set up to handle her multiple disabilities. I respected their opinion and their concern, but it still hurt every time they said it. I could not stand the thought of putting Nikki in a home like that, separating her from the family who loved and protected her. I continually came up with reasons why I could not do that, and the people at the regional center seemed to understand.

When Nikki reached puberty, and her behavior became drastically worse, I realized it was time to face the facts. After a lot of emotional turmoil, I called our caseworker and let her know we were ready to consider the possibility of placing Nikki in a group home. Even though I knew the waiting list would be long, I gave the caseworker the near-impossible parameters that I would accept. I told her Nikki's placement could not be located more than forty-five minutes away from our home, knowing this was a nearly impossible request for our area. The need was there, but the facilities were not.

A couple of weeks later, I got a call. Our caseworker told me she had found a possible placement for Nikki. I was shocked. I knew this was a come-to-Jesus moment. She went on to tell me that it was a wonderful home, located just forty-five minutes away.

"I don't think I'm ready," I confessed.

"Just go look at it. No commitment," she said. "You can arrange a trial weekend to see how Nikki does."

Steve and I discussed the pros and cons of the opportunity, and we decided to go and check the place out. I timed the drive and it took exactly forty-five minutes to get there. One minute longer would have been a deal breaker.

It was a beautiful, ranch-style home, clean and efficiently organized. That was already more than I could say for our own home. Friendly and professional staff showed us around and introduced us to the residents. An adorable girl, a little younger than Nikki, ran up to me, jumped into my arms, and gave me an intense hug. I was very touched and asked the caregiver about the child's situation. She told me that the girl's mom and dad had divorced and her autistic behavior was making it too hard for her mom, as a single parent, to keep her at home. She added that I resembled the girl's mother, which no doubt accounted for her attraction to me.

Impulsively I turned to Steve and asked if we could adopt her. He reminded me of why we were applying to the home in the first place. "Adoption is not an option, Jeanie. Not for us. Not after all that's brought us to where we are right now."

"I know. And you're right. Just thought I'd ask."

Steve smiled good-naturedly, and shook his head. The conversation was over.

After the tour, we decided to give the home a two-day` trial. We took Nikki there the following weekend, and we returned home looking forward to a break from our constant role as caregivers. Not nearly as relaxed as I had hoped to be, I found myself worrying about her day and night; I even found comfort in sleeping in her bed.

Are they watching her carefully enough? Is she getting her meds on time? Are they tucking her in at night with kisses and hugs? She needs those kisses and hugs.

At the end of what felt like a very long weekend, I could hardly wait to go and get her. Steve and I drove there on Sunday afternoon. They told us Nikki had done fine, but that she had a tendency to wander at night. "We found her diving headfirst into the refrigerator grabbing for a cube of butter."

No surprise there. I must have assumed they would have a gate on the bedroom door and a lock on the refrigerator, like we did at home.

As we sat at the kitchen table with Nikki, the staff began talking logistics with us. Nikki signed for a drink and a staff member got up to make her favorite, a glass of chocolate milk. I watched closely and took notes. I was not used to others attending to my daughter's needs.

Later, as we were driving home with Nikki, Steve asked me what I had thought of the home. Choking back tears, I said, "They put too much chocolate in her chocolate milk."

That said it all. I wasn't ready.

❖ ❖ ❖

Steve and Brian were going to the air show. It wasn't a Nikki-friendly outing, so she and I stayed home. Over the next few hours, Nikki paced endlessly around the backyard. I wished that she would stay in one place for a while, but that rarely happened. My plan was to let her get in the hot tub (one of her favorite pastimes) later in the day, close to the time the guys would get home. I had learned from experience that getting Nikki out of the hot tub was a two-person job, so I would have to wait for reinforcements. Yet, Nikki was bored and wanted in the tub now. She kept grabbing my hand, and walking me over to the hot tub, gesturing for me to take off the cover.

I signed to her, "Later."

Undeterred, she went into the house and came out carrying her swimsuit.

I signed, "I know. I understand. But we have to wait."

That was not the response she was going for. Her agitation button was getting close to sounding its alarm, which was never a good thing. Plopping herself on top of the hot tub cover, she sat cross-legged, her arms folded in anger. Just as I was considering the possibility of letting her go in earlier than I had planned, she arched herself backward and fell headfirst into the narrow space between the hot tub and the cement retaining wall. Her face squashed up against the cement as she slid down the wall, inching ever closer to the cement patio.

I ran to her as fast as I could, grabbed hold of the back straps of her overalls, and tried to pull her up. She was wedged in place, momentarily held up by her stomach. If she wiggled at all, she would slide down further and land hard on her head. I was a fairly strong person, but I was no match for the combined effects of her weight plus gravity. I also knew I could not let go, no matter what. But how long did I have before the straps broke?

For the first time in my life, I began yelling for help. Someone in the neighborhood would certainly hear me. I continued to yell, even louder, but no one came. My heart fell, as I realized I was totally on my own. I needed to stop and think.

Without changing the position of my arm that was holding Nikki in

place, I maneuvered myself up onto the hot tub cover, put my feet up against the cement wall, and gave it everything I had left in me. I had to pull her slowly, as her face was scratching against the rough cement. For the next twenty minutes as she cried and squirmed, I continued to tug carefully, making slow but steady progress.

In the end, Nikki came through this with no more than a few scrapes on her nose and forehead. I, however, was a total mess. I was lightheaded and really needed to sit for a while. Of course, Nikki had other plans. She started signing, "water" over and over again, until she was actually pounding her chin. I didn't have the stamina to hold out any longer.

"Fine, you win!" I yelled.

We both got into the hot tub, and stayed there for hours, until Steve and Brian finally came home. This time, they not only had to get her out; they had to help me out, as well.

✦ ✦ ✦

We were constantly adjusting Nikki's seizure medications based on her breakthrough seizure activity, blood levels, and alertness. Trying to balance these three important factors was a never-ending struggle. We found that some of the medications were antagonistic to one other, always battling for dominance in her bloodstream.

When Nikki began throwing up one day, our first guess was she had the flu or a virus. That assumption led to multiple trips to the doctor's office without finding any other symptoms of illness. Her blood levels seemed fine and, most of the time, she acted as though she felt fine. Soon, however, her throwing up became a daily occurrence. She was missing a lot of school and stumping her doctors.

Nikki was now scheduled to see a gastroenterologist. I thought maybe all of her seizure medications could have caused an ulcer. I knew they could act like battery acid to the stomach lining. This referral led to many lengthy and unpleasant tests, but still no answers. Every time Nikki threw up at school or at SHARP, they called me at work to come and pick her up. The policy was that she was not to return to school the following day, to prevent the spread of any potential germs. While I understood that policy, it didn't make it any easier on Nikki, my employer, my coworkers, or me. All the time I stayed home with her under these circumstances, she generally felt fine and never failed to remind me how bored she was, and how much she wanted to get out of the house. She eventually started to put her hand down her throat, causing herself to throw up. Was this a new, disgusting behavior or was she aware enough to know that she felt sick, and that this would make her feel better?

If only she could tell me.

As with so many things before, this behavior became our new normal. Out of necessity, I started keeping a box of gallon-size plastic bags in the car. When Nikki began making her precursor sounds while we were driving, I would nonchalantly pull out one of the bags, lean back, let her throw up in it, zip it up, and just keep on driving. When I reached the next pull-off point, I would clean her up and throw away the bag. Off we would go again, as though nothing had happened–except that I knew she could not go on like this. We would have to figure it out.

My best guess was that if nothing else was wrong with her, the vomiting had to be related to the cocktail of medications she was on. The previous year, we had gone to our second conference on TS. I remembered meeting one of the guest speakers who was a doctor from a distinguished university in North Carolina who discussed the many new seizure medications on the market and the pros and cons of each of them. She had a captive audience, as everyone in attendance had been dealing with seizures. I remembered being impressed with her knowledge and her very approachable manner. Before the conference was over, I picked up her contact information to add to my resource binder.

What did I have to lose by trying to contact her? I knew it was a long shot, but it was worth a try. I found her card and called, expecting to get a receptionist or voice mail. To my extreme surprise, she answered the phone herself. I introduced myself, telling her that I had heard her speak at the conference and had taken her contact information before leaving.

"I cannot tell you how happy I am to be talking with you. I'm at my wit's end."

"Go on," she said.

I gave her a quick summary of what we had been going through and of my suspicions regarding Nikki's meds.

She graciously said, "Your timing is excellent. I actually have time now, if you would like to explain in detail what's been going on."

I settled in for a long conversation and gave her the list of seizure medications Nikki was taking. Then, starting from the beginning, I described our long, frustrating journey with the nonstop throwing up and told her how long it had been going on.

She listened to the details of the symptoms I described and, after a few moments, she said, "You know, I might have an idea for you. It could be a shot in the dark, but I think it s worth pursuing."

My ears perked up. "I'm listening."

She told me about a patient who had recently come to her with a similar problem. He was a lawyer in his forties with a seizure disorder who had been on the same combination of Depakote and Dilantin, as Nikki. As his doctor adjusted the dose of each drug, he had begun to show serious side effects that eventually left him debilitated. He had reached a point where he could no longer work or take care of himself. His blood levels had all tested in the normal range, but something was drastically wrong. She advised his doctors to order a special test for determining the level of "free" Dilantin in his blood, which came in at a highly toxic level. The medicine he had been taking to help control his seizures had been slowly but surely poisoning him. After a change in medications, he eventually returned to normal and was able to go back to work.

Since Nikki seemed to be in a similar situation, this specialist recommended I ask Nikki's doctor to order the same "free" Dilantin blood test right away. She gave me all the relevant details of the test, and instructed me that the blood be sent to the specialty lab she used for her own patients. She said she would watch for the results.

When I discussed all of this with Nikki's neurologist, he said he was not familiar with this particular blood test. "Besides, he said, "your insurance won't pay for it."

So what were my options? Let Nikki just keep throwing up every day, or pay for a single blood test that might help her? I told him I wanted the blood test. The doctor agreed to do it, but he didn't like the fact that I was questioning his judgment.

Oh, well. You have to do what you have to do.

The blood was drawn and sent to the specialty lab. Four days later, the doctor from North Carolina called to tell me her hunch had been correct. Nikki, too, was toxic on Dilantin.

"This explains why your daughter's been constantly throwing up."

The news made me feel so sick to my stomach, I wanted to throw up.

"In other words, we have been unknowingly poisoning her. The poor thing! All that time she wasn't able to tell us how sick she was feeling."

"Exactly. I am so glad you came to me with this problem. Now it can so easily be remedied."

When Nikki's neurologist saw the results of the blood test, he reluctantly began to transition her to a new seizure medication. The vomiting came to a stop.

I remember the first day that she didn't throw up as clearly as if it were yesterday. It was a Super Bowl Sunday and we, as a family, were in a festive mood. Unlike most families, our celebration that day had nothing to do with football. Instead, it was all about celebrating the end of our year-long ordeal.

✦ ✦ ✦

In her teens, Nikki's weight increased and her feet began to turn under—not a good combination. She walked on the outside edges of her shoes, and she became prone to spraining her ankles. I made an appointment with the local podiatrist to find out what we could do about this situation. This led us to an appointment with another specialist and x-rays of her feet. After months of consultations, the doctor decided that a neurological problem was at the root of these orthopedic side effects.

Oh good, another visit to a neurologist. My favorite.

The podiatrist referred Nikki to a renowned specialist at an even more renowned medical center. We drove hours north again, hoping for answers.

138   M O M M Y   M O V E   T H E   S U N

After waiting for over an hour-and-a-half, we were greeted by a medical student who came in and spent thirty minutes asking us questions and taking notes. Then the student left and forty-five minutes later, the doctor came in. He looked at Nikki and told her to get up on the table. When she didn't respond, he looked frustrated.

I told him Nikki was deaf. "We use sign language to communicate with her."

He surprised me by saying, "Okay. Then sign to her to get up and walk out of the room."

"Well, that's not part of her routine. She won't understand that."

Under his breath he muttered, "I thought so."

"You thought what?" I asked, calling him on his sarcasm.

He ignored me, but I went on anyway. I told him the steps we had taken to figure out why her feet were turning under, and then I asked him, "What can be done to help her?"

His answer was cold and impersonal. "Due to her compromised brain function, the nerves are not communicating properly with the muscles, tendons, and ligaments in the outside of her legs and feet. That's what causes them to turn under. It's not that uncommon in people like this."

I ignored yet another rude comment from him, and pushed on. "Would braces help to correct it? Does she need surgery?"

That's when he said the words that still echo in my brain: "To be honest with you, she is not worth fixing."

The wind was knocked out of me by his callousness. After a few moments, once I was able to catch my breath, I asked him, "How can you be so cruel? My daughter is a human being."

His answer was characteristically abrupt, "My job is to be a realist."

I got up, grabbed Nikki's hand, and, together, we walked out of there. I didn't cry this time. I was slowly becoming hardened to the insensitive abuse we would get from certain elitists in the medical profession. It was another long drive home, quiet and sobering.

That evening, I was still so upset by the treatment we had received that I called my friend who also had a disabled son. I needed to talk with someone who understood where I, as a mom, was coming from. She told me her son had been referred to the same doctor, and that he had been just as blunt and unfeeling with them. Like us, they had refused to go back to him. I hated to hear that someone else had been spoken to in that way. However, it helped me confirm that I wasn't just being overly sensitive. I couldn't help but wonder if these doctors would speak in the same way if they had similarly disabled children.

I went back to our podiatrist and asked for a prescription for a buildup to the outside of each of Nikki's orthopedic shoes. I figured the buildups would stop her ankles from turning under when she walked. The adjustment worked, and she's been wearing them ever since. Some shoes, of course, are more buildup-friendly than others, depending on their design and the material they are made of. Fortunately for Nikki, she isn't too picky about her shoe styles.

✦ ✦ ✦

It was a cold and rainy night. Brian was at the middle school refereeing a basketball game, and Nikki and I were to pick him up by 6 p.m.. Nikki had just finished her dinner and was getting a little agitated. I struggled to put her raincoat on over her pajamas and then get her into her slippers. We had to go. At least the middle school was close to home.

As we pulled up in front of the school, I stopped a few feet from the door and ran in to get Brian's attention. I wanted to let him know we were there and that I would be waiting outside for him. In less than a minute, I was headed back toward the van when suddenly I heard a loud crash, followed by the sight of glass raining down in front of me. Our van's windshield had shattered into thousands of tiny pieces, and there was a huge, gaping hole where it once had been. I could see Nikki sitting in the front seat, covered in glass shards. She looked just as stunned as I was feeling.

With my heart racing, I immediately opened the door and began carefully brushing away fragments of glass from every inch of her. I pulled her out of the car and checked her for injuries, relieved to find nothing major. I did notice her bare right foot was now serving as a pincushion for countless numbers of glass particles. That was when I realized Nikki's slipper had come off, and that she had somehow managed to kick the windshield with her bare foot. Unil then, I didn't even know it was possible to break windshield glass that way. Moving quickly, I put her into the backseat, hooked up her seat belt, ran back into the school to arrange a ride for Brian, and drove straight toward home.

As I drove, I was pelted by raindrops and bits of glass. I couldn't see much, as I was looking through the jagged hole in a windshield that continued to crumble as I drove.

Thank God, we don't live far away.

When we got home, I grabbed Nikki from the backseat and struggled to carry her up the steep driveway to our house. This was no easy task, as she weighed more than I did, but I couldn't let her walk with the glass still stuck in her foot. Once I got her inside, I stripped off her clothes, and searched her from head to toe for any cuts or glass splinters. Amazingly, she was fine except for the glass I was able to extract from her right heel with tweezers. It looked as though the funky raincoat she was wearing had saved her. At that moment, it was worth its weight in gold.

A few minutes later, I heard a car pull up outside and knew it had to be Brian. He spotted the damage to the van and ran up the driveway with a horrified look on his face. He yelled, "Is Nikki okay? What happened?"

Before I could open my mouth, Nikki came bounding out, stark naked, to greet him with a huge smile on her face. He turned to me, dumbfounded.

"Don't ask!" I warned him.

After I got Nikki back into her PJs and ready for bed, I sat down with Brian and recounted the horrible details of the evening. As usual, she was fine and I was the one trying to recover.

✦ ✦ ✦

On another weekend afternoon, Steve came outside to take over Nikki patrol while I went to the store. We had passed the baton and he was getting settled outside as I was heading out the door. A millisecond before the front door clicked shut I heard a loud crash followed by the shattering of glass, followed by Nikki's screaming. I ran to the backyard, only to find her with blood oozing down her arm and her hand. I couldn't tell how badly she was hurt, but I knew it was serious. She had two extremely deep cuts.

Steve yelled, "Run in and get towels!"

I complied, double-time. He took the two towels I had brought out to him, wrapped one tightly around her hand and the other around her forearm. Then he picked her up and we all ran to the car. I held Nikki tight in the backseat as Steve drove to the emergency room, a route that was all too familiar.

When we arrived, we found that many people had gotten there ahead of us so we had to play the wretched waiting game. While we sat there watching the clock, the staff brought us new towels to replace the ones that had become soaked with blood and began to drip onto the floor.

"That's it? That's all you can do to help us?" I asked.

About halfway through the wait, they finally gave Nikki a Valium. I could use some too, I thought.

Three hours later, Nikki had to have a large part of her thumb stitched back into place, and she was now missing a two- by-four-inch chunk of tissue from her forearm. There was nothing left to stitch back onto it; her arm would simply have to heal from the inside out. The doctor said she might need plastic surgery to close up the wound.

Then it became another waiting game. Every day for the next six weeks, Wendy and I took Nikki to the doctor during my lunch hour, so he could change the bandages and check for infection. This was a long six weeks, as keeping Nikki from disturbing her bandages and impeding her healing was no easy task. She also pleaded with us every evening for her tubby time and we would have to continually sign "no". This made her very unhappy, and our evenings very difficult. Her wounds finally healed on their own, but they left visable scars on her and emotional scars on all of us. After this ordeal, Steve and I had all our windows covered with safety film, so this could never happen again.

✦ ✦ ✦

Nikki and I were going to pick up Brian from his summer basketball camp in San Jose. Since I knew the way, the family of one of his teammates had decided to follow us.

We started out with Nikki happily and safely buckled up in the back-seat of our van. For over an hour, everything was going along fine. Once we were on the freeway, Nikki started getting wound up. Within seconds, she had inched her way out from under the seat belt. Her foot accidentally pushed my rolled up yoga mat that was between the front seats, jamming it forward against the accelerator. We lurched forward at high speed with traffic surrounding us on all sides. I thought we were going to die.

Wait! We can't die. We have people following us.

With one hand grasping the steering wheel and the other tugging on the yoga mat to dislodge it from the gas pedal, I was finally able to slow the van down. After letting out a premature sigh of relief, I saw Nikki lunge suddenly at the door handle and I heard the door unlock. I also heard my-self scream.

Oh, my God…NO!

I pulled off the freeway, spraying gravel in all directions, and slammed the van into park. The teammate's dad also stopped and came running up to see if we were okay.

"That was some erratic driving back there," he said.

"No shit," I said. "We're lucky to be alive."

I was shaken to the core but he still expected me to lead them to the basketball camp.

Breathe, Jeanie, breathe!

We finally made it there safely, but I was still shaking as we drove up. It wasn't until Brian got in the van, that I was finally able to calm down. Being Nikki's brother, he has always understood, more so than anyone else. As I was describing our scary drive to him, it occurred to me just how close of a call it had actually been. In retrospect, I was hoping we all had nine lives like a cat, because we were seriously pushing the envelope.

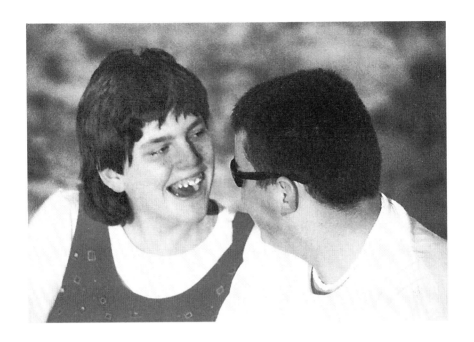

PART FIVE
✦
NIKKI: AGE 15 - 18

HER HIGH SCHOOL YEARS

By the time Nikki was ready for the secondary phase of her education, our local high school had just opened a special education classroom. It was twice as thrilling for us as a family, as Brian was attending the same high school.

The new special education teacher seemed to be a positive advocate for the students. Plus, Nikki had a wonderful one-on-one aide, and seeing them together was always heartwarming. The aide was a very petite woman, and looked even more so next to Nikki, who was twice her size. It was obvious that Nikki loved her and that the feeling was mutual. She could get Nikki to do anything she asked. Brian would often tell me he had seen them walking around campus together–Nikki doing her happy-hop. That said it all! Brian introduced Nikki and her classmates to his friends, and the whole student body began to welcome them. Always the devoted brother, Brian walked Nikki around campus on his lunch break, and he even sent flowers to the girls in her class on Valentine's Day. Because of his efforts, Nikki and her classmates were accepted and appreciated at the school.

All this positive momentum almost came to an abrupt halt with one phone call from Nikki's teacher. He informed me he needed to meet with me, but wouldn't say why. Naturally, I wasn't getting a good feeling, so I called Doug Brown and asked if he could attend the meeting. I also requested that Nikki's aide be invited and made arrangements for Brian to get out of class to join us. On the day of the meeting, I left work with butterflies in my stomach, as I had no idea what was coming. When I arrived at the school, I saw Brian with Nikki's teacher outside her classroom. That seemed like a good sign, but by the time I had grabbed my things and locked the car, Brian was walking off with his head hanging down. He was out of earshot, but the teacher wasn't, so I asked him, "What just happened out there?"

"I told Brian he was not invited to the meeting, as he had nothing to do with the outcome, and that he should go back to class."

I countered. "He has every right to be there. I already made all of the necessary arrangements."

"And I superseded them. I don't want him to hear what I'm going to tell you."

I couldn't believe what I had just heard. Butterflies, hell! Now I was enraged. We walked to the meeting room in total silence. With each step, I could feel my blood pressure rising. As we entered the meeting room, I was relieved to see that Doug and Nikki's aide were already there. The teacher began the meeting by saying he was just going to cut to the chase. He felt strongly that Nikki's functioning level and her behavior were inappropriate for his classroom activities and he wanted her out! I felt I had been kicked in the stomach. The tears erupted. He stopped talking long enough for me to find a box of tissues and then continued to make his case.

Nikki's aide and I took turns pulling tissues out of the box and wiping our drippy eyes and noses. I was now in no condition to make a convincing and effective rebuttal.

At that point, Doug took over the meeting and told the teacher that we would look into our options and reminded him of his limited authority. "You must realize you are not solely in charge of Nikki's placement. We will get back to you with our recommendations."

In the meantime, Nikki's aide would assume full responsibility for her care. At that point, it was time for me to leave. Nikki's aide and I had emptied the entire box of tissues. My eyes were still puffy and my nose was red when I left the room. Unfortunately, I bumped into one of Brian's friends from the varsity football team in the hallway. Self-conscious about my appearance, I put my head down and kept walking, hoping he wouldn't take notice and report to Brian what he had seen. I consoled myself by rationalizing that he was a high school boy with a lot of other things on his mind. I knew Brian was already upset from what Nikki's teacher had told him. If he knew I was a mess from the results of the meeting, he would feel even worse.

Wearing a fake smile, I forced myself to go to the game that night. As I watched Brian play, my mom instincts told me my son was not okay. He finished the game, but he just wasn't himself. He didn't even leave the field with his teammates. After seeing him take off his helmet and walk towards the goalposts alone, I ran down onto the field. When I caught up to him, I saw he had tears in his eyes so I hugged his tall, sweaty self and asked if he was sad about losing the game.

He said, "What game? What I need to know is what happened at that meeting? My friend told me he saw you looking extremely upset afterward, and, Mom, Nikki's teacher wouldn't even let me be there."

I tried to reassure him that everything would be okay. We held each other for a long time. The question occurred to me; how many varsity football players out there would put the feelings of their sister and mom ahead of their own during an important football game? I can't answer that question, but I'm still in awe of Brian.

Nikki finished the year in her class at the high school. The only other option for her at that point was what I called a "parked classroom." I wouldn't do that to her. She was still loved by her aide and her classmates, and the teacher didn't have to deal with her much. Ironically, that teacher was gone the following year, for reasons I can't recall, and Nikki was welcomed and embraced by his replacement. That next year went much more smoothly, and Nikki still had the same loving aide. With Brian off at college by then, I made more house calls to see how Nikki was doing.

✦ ✦ ✦

After months of filling out applications, we had been accepted by a program that offered us one respite weekend a month from Nikki's constant care, something much needed and truly appreciated. The plan was for me to drive Nikki to the program's facility in Santa Cruz on Friday evenings and then pick her up on Sunday afternoons. The facility was staffed for between five and eight clients. We had heard nothing but good reviews about the care provided there, so we felt comfortable leaving Nikki with them. There were activities and outings planned for each weekend, and most importantly, there were safety locks and buzzers on all the doors. Nikki attended five of these weekends and she always seemed happy when we picked her up. What a great find! Those free nights were golden to us, and they were fun for Nikki, too.

Then, one weekend, we got a call. Nikki had somehow pulled a Houdini and managed to get out of the facility. She was discovered walking down a busy street alone. Once again, a kind passerby sensed that something was off and interceded. Familiar with the weekend program, she walked Nikki back to the facility before the staff even realized she was gone. Something I did not enjoy hearing. Upon investigation, we found out that the buzzers on the outside doors had been out of order, and yet the facility staff hadn't thought it worth mentioning.

So much for respite weekends. It was great while it lasted.

THAT'S OUR POLICY

Sometimes in the car, Nikki's agitated states would erupt, out of nowhere, into rage-fits. Remember the deadly yoga mat? She would flail around until she was able to slide out from beneath her seatbelt–a technique she had honed to perfection. Once, she managed to kick the automatic gearshift into reverse while I was going seventy-five miles an hour on the freeway. There were also times when Nikki would reach forward and grab my hands off the steering wheel. Sometimes, she would grab my neck and pull it back, or she would hit me in the head with her hard plastic mirror, all while fastened in her seatbelt. I'm still not sure how we all came out of these situations alive. There were too many dangerous experiences, and I knew I had to do what I could to keep them from happening in the future. We had been lucky so far, but we had to stop tempting fate.

Nikki's actions were never intentional. Each time they occurred, we knew she was in an unexplained altered state. And no one knew for sure what triggered it. Was it her medications? The seizure activity? Behavioral outbursts? I knew she was not to blame. I just needed to keep Nikki and my family safe.

I spoke with Nikki's school bus drivers about the different types of seatbelt restraints they used in their vehicles. They showed me several different options. I liked the one that clipped at the shoulders as well as the waist; it looked safe and comfortable. Maybe this was the solution to our problem. I researched the Internet and found an identical seatbelt for sale. Then I contacted our regional center, which helped fund the equipment needed to keep its clients safe in their home environments, and I submitted a funding request.

Before the staff at the center could fill my order, they required that I be interviewed by their psychologist. They needed to know why I wanted to restrain my daughter and to verify that I had her best interests at heart. During the interview, I explained our near-miss experiences while driving, and I assured the psychologist that my intention was to keep my daughter and the rest of my family alive. I passed with flying colors. Once I jumped through their hoops, I thought we could get down to business. I told them the seatbelt I wanted was available online from a Florida distributor for under $300. They responded "unfortunately, we won't be able to order from them since we are not authorized to purchase from that company. We have a vendor we use who carries a similar product."

Being a bottom-line type of person, I asked, "What does your vendor charge for the item?"

When they looked on the price sheet, we were all surprised to see that the same seatbelt, from their vendor, cost just under $1,000. I was shocked.

"Don't you think that is a waste of the state's resources?" I asked.

"Well, that is our policy," they said.

✦ ✦ ✦

And then there was the time I wanted to change Nikki's monthly diaper order from size medium to large. I thought it would be a simple adjustment. Well, I thought wrong.

The battle began with my first phone call to the medical supply agency. They told me that to change our order I would need to get a new prescription for the larger size diaper and a letter from Nikki's doctor explaining why the change was necessary.

Shouldn't the reason be self-explanatory? Okay, play their little game, Jeanie.

At the time, Nikki's doctor was on vacation for two weeks but, no problem as he had partners. But another waiting game was required after I found out the agency would only accept a letter from the doctor listed on the original prescription. We would just have to buy the much more expensive diapers for the next few weeks. This wouldn't be too bad in the grand scheme of things.

When the doctor got back, I called and made arrangements for him to send the new prescription and the letter to the agency. After enough time had passed for it to arrive, I called the medical supply agency to verify that they had what they needed now and would process the order. The good news was they had the prescription and the doctor's letter. The bad news? They told me I would need to get another denial letter from our insurance company, explaining that they would not cover the cost of the larger-sized diapers.

"Your order cannot be processed until we have a new denial letter. That is our policy."

This meant making another agonizing call to the insurance company, navigating their user-unfriendly maze of automation, and waiting for that elusive human being to answer. "Your call is important to us. Please hold the line and someone will be with you shortly." If I had a dollar for each time I've heard that recording over the years, I would be long since retired.

When the live voice finally came on the line, I explained the situation and asked if she could please send a new denial letter. Of course, she couldn't do that without a letter addressed specifically from the doctor prescribing the larger diapers.

"What? You have to be kidding."

"That is our policy," I heard again.

The doctor and I were both getting frustrated. He agreed to send another letter to the insurance company. This was before emails and faxes were in widespread use, so I had to wait a few days for the letter to arrive. When I called, I got on the same automated hamster wheel that goes round and round, never getting you to exactly where you want to be.

Oh yes, they had the letter; but they had another hoop for me to jump through. The insurance company couldn't send a denial letter until they got an order from the supplier. They needed something tangible to deny.

With my blood pressure escalating, I knew I had to control my frustration and anger. Hold it in, hold it in, I kept telling myself, as I called the supply agency and navigated their maze of recorded options. As much as I needed to talk to a person, once again, I was placed in the inevitable "hold" mode.

Nikki's not the only one in the family who hates to wait. Heaven knows I've done enough of it these past few years and it never gets easier.

When a person finally came on the line, I pleaded with her to process an order for these diapers so the insurance company could send them the denial letter they needed. I told the person that this little request would make everybody happy, and we could get the much-needed diapers.

"I'm sorry, but we cannot process an order without first having a denial letter."

I tried to keep cool, but it was almost impossible. So I spoke slowly. "As I just mentioned to you, the insurance company first needs the denial letter in order to move forward. That is their policy."

"I'm sorry, ma'am. Perhaps you misunderstood. We cannot process an order without the denial letter. That is *our* policy."

That was it. I couldn't take it anymore. "May I please speak with your supervisor...? And now!"

She responded by putting me back on hold. The supervisor finally came on the line and I repeated the same story.

Her reply was the standard denial, adding, "That is our policy."

I came dangerously close to telling her to stick her policy where the sun doesn't shine. I was so angry, I was actually getting a visual, and it wasn't pretty. I forced myself to take a few deep breaths and explained everything I'd been through up to this point, only to still be without the diapers. I took her name and insisted on having her direct phone number. All I could think to do was to go back to the insurance company, get hold of a supervisor there, and set up a three-way conference call among all of us. That would be one interesting conversation, I thought.

It took me a week to do it, but I got both supervisors on the line. I began by explaining my dilemma with their opposing policies, and then I asked them to please discuss how they could compromise so the diaper order could be processed. They sounded like two spoiled brats fighting over a lollipop–shifting responsibility back and forth, back and forth. It was like witnessing an exhausting verbal tennis match, with no one claiming the coveted trophy.

Finally, I broke into the conversation. "Stop and listen to yourselves. We are getting nowhere. From where I stand, this discussion is a pathetic exercise in how to cover your asses. And, think about it. That's literally all I'm trying to do. Cover my daughter's growing ass."

That quieted them down for a few seconds before they started attacking each other again.

I told them, "We're not hanging up until one of you takes the first step toward ending this nonsensical standoff."

The supply supervisor finally, grudgingly, agreed to send an order request to the insurance supervisor. She sounded completely defeated. "It will take some time, but I'll get it done."

Hallelujah! I thanked her for being the bigger person, and asked that she send me a copy of the order, as well.

When the letter finally showed up in the mailbox, I felt a sense of relief as I opened it, dated it, and put it in Nikki's medical file. It was the order we needed for incontinence supplies. I called the insurance supervisor to make sure she had this important letter in her hot little hands and was ready to expedite the order. Oh, she had it all right; however, there was still a problem. The order had to be specifically for diapers. The term "incontinence supplies" was apparently too general for them. That terminology simply did not work for insurance companies. You have to be precise. "You understand," she said. "It's our policy."

I could not believe this was really happening. Was Candid Camera hiding in corners somewhere, following me around? I wished that were the case. Maybe some of the royalties would have reimbursed me for those months of being forced to purchase unnecessarily expensive diapers. After many more calls and weeks of waiting, the revised order finally arrived. No, of course this story isn't over. This time, the order was for–huh?–contact lenses. Unbelievable! There is only so much a human being can be expected to take, and, by that time, I had way exceeded my limit. From that moment on, my phone calls to the insurance company and the medical supply agency bordered on the hostile, but, in the end, I prevailed.

The simple task of changing diaper sizes had turned into an expensive, six-month battle filled with bureaucratic roadblocks. I felt I had aged significantly during the process. For the first time in my life, my doctor was concerned about my previously low blood pressure that was now sky-high.

"Anything stressful going on in your life? I mean, anything other than the usual?" he asked.

"You have no idea," I said, shaking my head.

My personal goal had always been to work *with* these agencies, not against them, as they control what we need for our children. Sometimes, though, they push you to the limit with senseless bureaucracy and then force you to use desperate measures. This was a classic example.

When the diapers finally came, I thought I had never seen anything as beautiful in my life. That night, our family actually celebrated their arrival. As I've already made clear, we don't do normal.

The next week, I decided to call the president of California's advocate agency for the disabled. I explained to him the unnecessary battles we were fighting every day for our kids and wanted him to understand that it was hard enough to meet their day-to-day needs. We didn't need to deal with these additional and completely unproductive roadblocks. He listened quietly to my entire story. When he finally spoke, it was the icing on the cake. "I'm so sorry…but these are our policies."

✦ ✦ ✦

When Nikki turned eighteen and became an adult in the eyes of the court system, things changed. We now had to deal with several more agencies—as if we weren't dealing with enough already. The biggest frustration was speaking with the representatives of these agencies at their limited convenience, and without them ever bothering to familiarize themselves with Nikki's case before contacting me. Their total disinterest required that I explain Nikki's condition over and over again to people who didn't understand her case, or didn't care enough to learn.

The most critical problem arose when I was no longer able to get her medical test results from the doctors. Since she was now considered an adult, Nikki needed to contact the doctors directly to authorize me to access her records. Yeah, right! When I explained the situation to these agencies, their responses were uniform, and always the same: "I'm sorry. That is the law."

Yes, I got it. The law is the law; no exceptions. But why did this apply as well with the doctors who had followed Nikki's health and known us since her birth? Under the circumstances, we were forced to hire a lawyer to set up a conservatorship for us, her parents, allowing us to make all the necessary decisions concerning her welfare. It was an extra expense and effort just to continue doing what we had been doing for the first eighteen years of her life. We were told that we had no option, and that we simply had to play along. Okay, fine. (*Fine* meaning: frustrated, insecure, neurotic, and emotional.) Were we really seeing our medical and legal systems at their best? What a scary thought.

The first step in the process was for Nikki to be interviewed by a court-appointed individual.

This ought to be good. Play along, Jeanie. You have no choice.

I made the appointment and realized that, in some warped way, I was actually looking forward to it. The interviewer, a young man who still looked wet behind the ears, walked into our living room. After we made all the pleasant introductions, he asked Steve and me to leave the room so he could talk privately with Nikki. We turned to each other, and smiled.

Sure, whatever you want.

After thirty seconds alone with Nikki, the young man called us back into the room. Yes, we had been timing him. His attitude was showing when he said to us, "I asked Nikki a question, and she refused to answer me. She would not even make eye contact. Can you explain why?"

Obviously, he hadn't done his homework, which we had suspected from the start.

"Hmmm, let me see," I said, thoroughly enjoying myself. "It might just be because she's deaf and doesn't speak. Or, maybe she just doesn't like you."

He looked puzzled, so Steve decided to let him off the hook, and fill him in on Nikki's condition—even though I was all for prolonging his discomfort just a bit longer.

We explained to him that we communicated with Nikki through basic sign language. It took him a while to get it, but he slowly came around.

He asked Steve to sign to Nikki, "Is it okay with you if your mom and I take care of you?"

Smirking, Steve played along. He signed the question to Nikki, and she responded with her universal sign for food. As usual, she had other priorities. No surprise to us.

"What did she say? How did she answer your question?"

Steve couldn't resist. He wasn't sure how long we could carry on with this absurd charade, but, like me, he wasn't yet ready to give it up. It was too good. With a straight face, he looked at the interviewer to be sure he had his attention, then back to Nikki, to whom he fake-signed, "If I've told you once, I've told you a million times. You are not going to move to Paris and share an apartment with Lindsay. End of discussion."

The look of total confusion on the face of the court representative was truly a Kodak moment. Talk about finding humor in an otherwise serious situation. I could no longer help but laugh out loud. The release felt so good. And once the barrier was broken, Steve could no longer hold back, either. Suffice it to say, the interviewer left that day without his answer. As for Steve and me, the episode considerably lifted our mood.

A week later, the court sent another, more seasoned, individual. She met Nikki briefly and proceeded to file the necessary paperwork. You would have thought that we had played Ring Around the Rosie enough after this first experience, but a couple of weeks later, we found that we still weren't done. A call came in from the court telling me that there was one more part to the process. It required that Nikki be interviewed by a psychologist from our regional center. I called our lawyer and told him about this additional hoop they wanted us to jump through. He said, "We all know it's ludicrous. Just humor them and go through the paces."

Okay, here we go again.

I made the appointment, and Wendy's daughter and I took Nikki to her interview in Salinas. As we were waiting to be called into the psychologist's office, Nikki began her familiar grunting and grabbed her tummy. We both knew exactly what this meant and started looking for the restroom. Just then, the door to the psychologist's office opened, and he asked us to come on in. We told him that we needed to take Nikki to the restroom first. His response was, "Oh, no; that can wait. This will only take a few minutes."

"But you don't understand," I said.

He walked over to Nikki, patted her on the back, and walked her into his office. "No problem," he said.

Oh, there's a problem all right, as you're about to find out.

Well, Nikki did the job we knew she had to do. After a moment, stuck in his clueless state, the psychologist mumbled something about a bad odor. Then he told Nikki to sit down, so they could talk. Of course, she didn't cooperate. The doctor looked frustrated, and asked me why she was behaving this way.

"Well, for one thing, as you know, she can't hear. She also doesn't like having to sit down when her diaper is full. May we please take her to the restroom now?"

"No. I have an appointment right after yours. So we need to get down to business." She just did, I thought to myself.

"All righty, then," I said.

"So, you said she's deaf?" he asked.

"Have you read her chart? I asked.

"Well, actually, I haven't had time."

Oh, this just keeps getting better.

I stared at him and said nothing.

"Okay, let's get down to business," he said, again. "Would you please sign to Nikki to pick up the toy on the table in front of her. I would like to see how she interacts with it."

Of course, Nikki had absolutely no interest in the toy, which was a boring, hard, gray metal object as opposed to her traditional preferences, which leaned toward the squiggly and colorful. She was also uncomfortable sitting in that pile of poop.

When it became obvious she had no intention of responding to the doctor's request, I spoke up. "As her mother, and based on my years of experience, I have to tell you she is far more likely to be cooperative once her diaper is changed."

Ignoring me, he continued to pursue his narrow agenda, which he soon saw for what it was: an exercise in futility. Finally he either reached the end of his professional rope or he could no longer tolerate the smell. "I do see that we're wasting time here. I would suggest you hurry along and change the child's diaper."

"Thank you."

He walked us to the restroom, and Wendy's daughter took Nikki inside to change her. The doctor took the opportunity to grill me with his standard questions. It seemed a long while before they returned, but when they did I could see that Nikki was feeling much better. I was certain that the doctor would now see he'd made the right decision. Instead, he turned to me with outstretched hand. "That will be all. Thank you for coming."

Confused, and yet relieved, I shook his hand and turned toward the exit. We walked out and laughed the whole way home about the stupidity of the process. These were the people making the legal decisions regarding our kids? The red tape over Nikki's conservatorship wound up taking nine frustrating months. When we were done, I had more gray hairs and more wrinkles, and we were $2,000 poorer. Ultimately, we played this elaborate game just to get back to where we had been in the first place.

✦ ✦ ✦

I can hardly wait to tell you about the time Nikki was called for jury duty. I had been asked to report for jury duty multiple times. But, as Nikki's primary caregiver, serving on a jury while taking care of her was not a viable option. Plus, getting last minute coverage for her was nearly impossible. Each time I was asked to report, in order to be excused, I had to request a signed letter from Nikki's pediatrician on his professional letterhead–no emails–to be sent to the courthouse. Over the years, this became a ritual. Since Nikki's condition was lifelong, wouldn't you think that one letter of explanation kept on permanent file would suffice into the future?

This particular story begins when Nikki, not I, got a letter to report for jury duty. Just picturing her in that scenario made me laugh. I was sure that one phone call to the courthouse would take care of the situation. Wrong again. The court clerk informed me they needed a letter from Nikki's doctor, verifying her disabling conditions.

"You should find an abundance of doctor letters in my file that will surely fulfill that requirement."

"Those are not applicable. Now that your daughter is an adult, she has her own file. It cannot be interchanged with yours. "

"She's still the same person, only a year older. Why all the additional work?"

"It's our policy."

And so we had to go through the entire lengthy and maddening procedure all over again. The doctor was as tired of writing letters as I was of asking him for them, so I tried faxing my copy of his most recent letter to the court. The clerk called and said, "A copy is not valid. We require an original signature."

Now I was frustrated. My sarcastic side started to surface and it projected onto the woman on the phone. I told her that I would bring Nikki to court, but she would have to arrange for someone to regularly check her diapers and administer seizure medications, as needed. There was dead silence on the other end of the line, so I broke the silence by adding that Nikki was also deaf, non-verbal, and functioned on the level of a two-year old with a very short attention span. The next words I heard were music to my ears.

"Oh, well, under those circumstances, I think this letter will suffice."

For the record, Nikki has never been called for jury duty again.

As an eighteen-year-old, Nikki became eligible for supplemental social security benefits. I made an appointment to apply for her and was told that Nikki's presence was required. After a long wait for the scheduled date, Nikki and I showed up and waited for our number to be called. I filled out volumes of forms and we waited some more. By the time the interviewer finally called us, I was exhausted from trying to keep Nikki seated. She found us with our legs intertwined—my last-ditch attempt to keep Nikki from getting up and walking off.

The interviewer started asking the required questions, but it threw her off when my answers didn't precisely match her forms. Little did she know that nothing about Nikki would fit a cookie-cutter form. After half an hour of questioning us, the woman leaned over to me and said, "Look, honey, you are far too honest to get the services that your daughter deserves. Trust me. You're going to have to start stretching the truth. They all do it, you know."

Welcome to another of our oh-so-accommodating bureaucratic agencies. I should have asked her if that was their policy.

CELEBRATIONS, WITH A NIKKI TWIST

For Nikki's eighteenth birthday, the staff at the resort where Steve was working, wanted to give Nikki a special gift: a day at the spa. We knew this would be a unique experience for everyone involved–unique being the operative word. However, if the staff was game to try it, so was I. Her spa treatment began with a warm bathtub full of bubbles, all sprinkled with rose petals. Nikki climbed in and plopped down with her usual grace, forcing the water to splash out on both sides of the tub and spill onto the floor. As she sat there covered in bubbles flicking water, I tried to soak up the overflow on the floor with any towels I could put my hands on. Once she decided she'd had enough soaking, Nikki jumped up and clambered out of the bathtub, spilling much of the remaining water onto the floor. With no towels left, I just wrapped her in the terry cloth robe and hoped for the best. As she walked out of the room, she left a trail of water and rose petals behind her. We were now on our way to her next spa treatment.

Outside on the patio, Nikki zeroed in on the hot tub and made a beeline in its direction. "Wait," I signed to her over and over.

I was trying to divert her attention to the pretty gazebo, where a man-icurist was waiting to give Nikki her first-ever pedicure. Nikki didn't quite get it. In her mind I assumed she was thinking, why would you want me to sit in that stupid chair when I could be happily seated in the hot tub flicking water?

As I maneuvered her past the hot tub and into the gazebo, she spotted the footbath filled with bubbly water positioned on the floor in front of the chair. No doubt, she thought that was better than nothing, and managed to plop her-

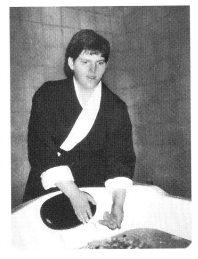

self into it. I wasn't sure how I was going to get her out of there and onto the chair now with the extra weight of her heavily soaked terrycloth bathrobe. It took both of us, the manicurist and me, to pull her out, and we ended up far more drenched than Nikki. An assistant quickly brought her another robe, and took away the wet one, wringing it out as she left.

Okay, let's try this again.

Nikki sat in the chair, with only her feet in the footbath this time. The patient manicurist began the pedicure process, but Nikki was just not into it. From her seat, she could see the edge of the hot tub, and it seemed to be calling her name. Nonetheless, she appeased us for a while, with a content look on her face as the manicurist began to paint her toenails. I finally began to relax and sat down with a magazine. Then, just as I turned the first page, Nikki lunged out of the chair and bolted towards the hot tub, her robe flying boldly behind her like Superman's cape. Neither of us could stop her. Nikki was on a mission to get into the hot tub, and she succeeded.

The manicurist observed pragmatically, "Well, I think our session is over." She handed me the hot-pink nail polish she had been using on Nikki's toenails. "Maybe you'll have better luck."

Needless to say, we had to wring out a second bathrobe. I think that might be a record for one spa visit.

✦ ✦ ✦

When it came time for our high school senior prom, Nikki and her classmates each received their own personal invitations. Things were changing for the better at our schools. Nikki hadn't been invited to a dance or a party since Steve took her to their father-daughter dance years back.

I was excited that Nikki and I would get to do all that special mom-and-daughter stuff. We planned to get her all glammed up for the big event. Dress? Check. Tights? Check. Hair accessories and makeup? Check. Wrist corsage? Double check. The big night was rapidly approaching, and Nikki would be ready to make her grand entrance.

Then I got a dreadful phone call. My dad in Oregon, who had been undergoing the ravages of chemotherapy, had taken a sudden turn for the worse. It was time for me to go up there. Okay, Jeanie, switch gears fast. I had to leave immediately, so I needed to make airline reservations in a hurry and pack a bag. I also needed to brief Steve and Brian on all the last-minute details for making Nikki prom-worthy. She felt the energy in the air, and knew that she was going to get dressed up and do something special. Naturally, she couldn't comprehend that my dad was sick, and I was not going to disappoint her by canceling her plans. Arrangements were already in place for Wendy to take Nikki and two of her friends to the prom and stay with them through the entire evening. For Steve and Brian, it was just a matter of getting Nikki ready. They understood how important this night was, not only for Nikki and her friends, but also for Brian's classmates, who had gone out of their way to personally invite them to the prom.

Before whisking me off to the airport, I got everything in place for my two guys. Since they were both basically clueless about the steps we women have to take to get ourselves ready for a special occasion, I had to explain what all the items were for, and how essential they all were to the final result.

"Mousse is for hair volume," I told Brian. "Please style her hair so it's feminine, and yet a little edgy."

He looked at me with a blank stare.

Then I had to show Steve which make-up was for her eyes, her cheeks, and her lips. He found another loose makeup item and asked, "What's this for?"

"If you don t know what it is, don't use it," I replied.

I assumed the clothes would be self-explanatory until they asked me whether they should put her tights on under or over her diaper. Oh, this was going to be good.

"Please guys, videotape this process for me," I said as I left. "I'm going to need a good laugh when I get back."

As soon as I arrived in Oregon, I settled in at the hospital with my dad and other family members, and I learned that there had been no change in his condition since the phone call. We tried to convince ourselves that this was a good sign. All we could do was wait and see.

Later that night, Steve called to tell me the girls had a great time. They had stayed at the prom the entire time and danced with the upperclassmen. No surprise that Nikki showed more interest in the vibrations from the large, stand-up speakers and chose to spend her time hugging them instead of dancing. Somehow, that didn't surprise me.

That's my girl!

The hours ticked by slowly at the hospital, and we were still holding onto hope. In the wee hours of the morning, however, we got the final word from the doctor. There was nothing more that could be done for my dad. The shock and the sadness were indescribable. Along with the rest of the family, I remained with him for his last few days. The following weeks were a total blur, as we went through the process of grieving together and making all the necessary arrangements. Losing my dad was very traumatic on the whole family.

It wasn't until I got home weeks later that I heard the whole story of Nikki's prom-night preparations. I had always known that humor was the best medicine, and it came to me in ample doses when I needed it the most.

This is how I heard the story from the experts, as they narrated the video for me. Steve and Brian had figured that their first task was to get Nikki into her tights, as those were the first item lined up on the bed. Brian held them up, looked at them, and then looked over at Nikki. He shook his head and said, "No way! There is a whole lot more of her than there is of these." Obviously, they were totally oblivious to that whole tummy-control thing and the tights' astonishing ability to stretch. Starting skeptically at Nikki's ankles, the guys worked their way up. Once they got close to the top, they each grabbed hold of one side of the tights and lifted her off the ground, shaking her all the way into them. She rewarded them by giggling with delight. After that ordeal, getting her into the red velvet dress seemed easy. They could tell Nikki was enjoying her special night. Maybe the prep would be the highlight—and maybe even more fun than the dance. With

Nikki, you never know.

Next came the makeup. A little blush here, there, and wherever.

"What's this again? Is this for her eyes?" Steve asked, staring at the mascara.

"Couldn't hurt," Brian agreed.

Nikki especially loved the lip gloss. Due to the heroic efforts of her dad and brother, they might even have managed to get some of it onto her lips. Okay. She had rosy cheeks, pretty eyes, and shiny lips. Now for the hair. Brian recalled my telling him that mousse equals volume. "Let's load her up!" he said.

He started by squirting a huge mound of it into his hand. Nikki immediately grabbed at the white foamy stuff and tried to eat it, logically mistaking it for whipped cream. Of course, with mousse on the loose, it ended up just about everywhere except in her hair.

"I guess we'll need more mousse," Brian said. "Let's just pile it on top of her head and go from there."

Fluff, sculpt, and style.

"Oh, wait! It still looks a little flat. Mom said she wanted volume."

"More mousse!" Steve and Brian cried out at the same time.

As the once full can sputtered the last few spurts of its contents, they decided this was as good as it was ever going to get. They both agreed Nikki looked beautiful–kind of. Their mission accomplished admirably, they felt proud of their good work. After giving her guys multiple hugs and kisses, Nikki turned around and headed for her bedroom.

At that point, Steve and Brian turned off the camera, and began cleaning up the mess.

Just minutes later, right before Wendy was due to arrive, they heard a loud thud.

"Uh-oh," Brian said to Steve. "That's not a good sound."

They ran down the hall to check on Nikki and found her plopped down on her waterbed with her dress pulled up over her tummy, which she was happily rubbing.

"She looked like a Buddha," they told me.

The back of her carefully coiffed hair was now smashed flat and standing up in the front like an ostrich plume.

"Ah, just a little touch-up and she'll be fine," Brian said.

Right then, the doorbell rang. "Timing is everything," they said. As Wendy walked in, she assessed the situation, and couldn't help but smirk. "Things going okay?" she asked skeptically.

"Don't ask!" they answered.

The instant the disheveled Nikki spied Wendy, she jumped up from her bed, and was ready to go. Wendy quickly took control of the situation and performed some minor damage control. For the final touch, she went to the refrigerator to get Nikki's wrist corsage, and then they were on their way.

According to their account of the story, once Nikki left for the evening, Brian and Steve just stood in place, trying to figure out what had just taken place. They needed to see it for themselves, so they watched the video several times over and laughed at it all the way through. Knowing how much I needed it, they couldn't wait to share it with me.

Now watching Nikki in the playback, I could see the twinkle in her eyes. She loved every minute of watching Steve and Brian trip all over themselves for her benefit. The video said it all. Thank heaven for technology, and for my two wonderful guys!

Sometimes, I think Nikki is sly like a fox. How many young girls do you know that get the undivided attention of their two favorite guys while getting primped for the prom? I believe she knows something we don't, and she always has.

✦ ✦ ✦

As Nikki approached the end of her last year in high school, a big decision had to be made. Most of the students in Nikki's class would automatically move on to our county's Transition Program. I had heard nothing but great things about it. Nikki, however, was at a lower functioning level than the program's staff was accustomed to teaching. There were very few alternatives to this program, and none that we felt good about. Wendy, one of Nikki's strongest advocates, did everything she could to convince the people at the program to accept Nikki, at least on a trial basis. She even

begged them to give Nikki a chance. It took some doing, but her persistence won out. Hallelujah! Nikki would be moving on to a great program with her friends.

What a year it had been for the special education class at the high school. First, the senior prom and now graduation. Out of her entire class, only four students would be moving on to the Transition Program in the fall and luckily one of them was Nikki. They were each invited to participate in the graduation ceremony with all of the other high school seniors. Brian had just finished his first year of college in Colorado and he flew home to escort his sister through the ceremony. I was thrilled and proud of both of them.

The big day came, and we were brimming with excitement. Nikki's cap and gown were pressed, her carnation lei ready, and she was wearing another new dress and matching tights. Brian took her to the school to help get her ready for the ceremony. Steve and I arrived at the outdoor stadium early to get good seats. I decided to sneak down to the classroom, just to see if Brian needed any help. When I walked in and saw my two kids together, standing hand in hand, my eyes welled up with happy tears. There was

Nikki, looking like a scholar in her cap and gown; and there was Brian, looking like her handsome personal FBI escort. A few of the other girls looked envious, and I even heard one of them say, "What do I have to do to get an escort like that?"

Brian had everything under control, so I went back to the stands to enjoy the ceremony. There I joined Nikki's amazing fan club. Family, friends, daycare providers, teachers, classmates–basically her entire circle of support, past and present, were there to cheer her on and share in the celebration.

My mom flew down from Oregon by herself. She and my dad, who had recently passed, had been planning to make the trip together, as they were both so proud of Brian and Nikki. The trip would now be bittersweet for her, but she wasn't going to let Nikki down. This was our girl's big moment.

The music started, and all eyes were on the graduates as they walked through the balloon arch. The excitement was contagious. Everybody was whooping and hollering. Nikki and Brian were in the middle of the pack. They made it to their seats uneventfully, and we all crossed our fingers that Nikki would make it through the entire ceremony without an incident. Since the sun was out and it was pleasantly warm, we had good reason for our high hopes.

For a while, Nikki sat there like a perfect lady. Then we could see her beginning to squirm. Brian calmly reached into his pocket and brought out a small mirror, which he handed to her. How smart he was! This held her interest for a good fifteen minutes. Then she noticed the reflection of the tassel on her cap, which intrigued her enough that she dropped the mirror and began flicking the tassel back and forth with her hand. Next, she started swinging her head from side to side so she could watch the tassel swishing past her face. Eventually, she got sleepy, leaned her head on Brian's shoulder, and fell asleep, content to be with her brother and feel the warm sun on her shoulders. This was a good sign. It looked as though she just might make it. As the speeches were coming to a close, and it was almost time for the graduates to start their procession across the stage to receive their diplomas, Brian gently nudged Nikki awake.

When Nikki's turn came, he took her hand and escorted her up onto the stage. When her name was called her entire fan club erupted into cheers, clapping, and waving. Steve even let out his signature war whoop that he had always reserved for Brian's football games. When Nikki looked up toward the stands and saw all of the people cheering, she began to smile and clap her hands.

What a ham! She's loving it!

As she descended the steps from the stage, I noticed she was walking a little differently. Uh-oh! I recognized that walk. Luckily, everyone else's eyes were focused on the next graduate crossing the stage. I got up quietly and met Brian and Nikki at the edge of the bleachers. After a quick hug and the exchange of a few code words, I whisked Nikki off to the restroom. By the time we got there, her diaper had slipped down around her ankles. We did a quick change, and we were still in time to meet everybody else on the field, right as the graduates threw their hats in the air. Of course, Nikki didn't want to part with hers, as she had grown quite fond of her tassel.

Brian later explained that her diaper had begun falling as she stepped onto the stage, and that, even as it was inching closer to her knees as they were stepping down from the stage, there was nothing he could have done to solve the problem. He simply held his breath and prayed that the tights would do their magic and that she wouldn't take a tumble. Afterward, we all went to the house for a truly joyous graduation party. Everyone commented on how well Nikki had done through the entire event. Brian and I just smiled at each other and nodded.

PART FIVE

✦

NIKKI: AGE 19 - PRESENT

NIKKI, ALL GROWN UP

Even though all classroom transitions were difficult, this one was going to be even harder. Wendy had done everything she possibly could
for Nikki; now it was up to Nikki to prove herself at her new program. It
wasn't easy at first. Nikki had always been a one-on-one student, and the
Transition Program was set up for three-on-one supervision. All of the staff
worked extra-hard to help Nikki succeed and before long they all caught the
highly contagious Nikki bug. The teacher, who had been the most hesitant
at first, now saw Nikki's potential. She worked extremely hard with her and
became another of her strong advocates. From that point on, Nikki was
officially part of the group. She liked being a team member, and she thrived
in this enriching and challenging environment. Along with the entire staff,
she took great pride in her accomplishments. And so did I.

When Nikki turned twenty-one, it was an especially exciting milestone.
We never thought she would live to see that day. We had to celebrate, to do
something extra-special.

After doing a lot of creative thinking, I came up with a plan. This celebration wouldn't be just for Nikki, it would also be for all the people who
had known and loved her. I went to her school and approached her teacher
with my idea. She loved it. This would be fun for her classmates, and it
would also be a great learning experience about restaurant etiquette and
proper manners. I just had to get all the players lined up, as this would definitely be a team effort.

We planned to turn the school's downstairs great room into Restaurante Dominique. Since Nikki's all-time favorite meal was our traditional
Thanksgiving dinner, that was what we would serve. The meal would need
to include both my mom's traditional stuffing and Steve's mom's sweet potatoes. They would have to travel from the Oregon coast and the Bay Area,
to make their specialties. We assigned the rest of the menu items to other
family members, and the plan was put into action.

The recipes were quadrupled for the thirty-plus expected guests, and the shopping lists were made. I created personal invitations and sent them to Nikki's classmates, teachers, aides, principals, and school staff. They would all be our guests at our fancy restaurant, and our family members would be the wait staff, complete with matching aprons. I designed and printed the menus, purchased the decorations, planned the matching dinnerware, and, of course, got champagne glasses for the sparkling apple juice toast. Brian flew home from college just to be part of this special celebration.

On the big day, we were all in the school kitchen putting the last-minute touches to the feast. The tables were set restaurant-style, with a menu at each place setting. Decorations were hung, flowers were on the tables, soft music was playing in the background, and Nikki's "Queen for the Day" throne was ready to receive her at the head of the table. The ambience we visualized had come to fruition, the food was ready, and the family wait staff was eager to serve. All dressed up for the occasion, the guests began entering our restaurant and were ushered to their tables. After they were all seated, we began pouring the sparkling apple juice into their champagne glasses for a toast to the birthday girl. After our family members had all made their speeches, we were pleasantly surprised by how many others stood up to give her a touching tribute.

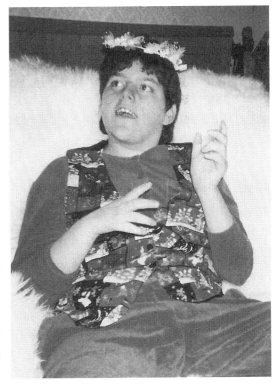

As the guests sat in eager anticipation, we began to serve the meal. They were all smiles and so appreciative. There were many thank-yous and thumbs-up as we made our way around the tables. I was amazed at how well behaved and polite the students were—better manners than I have sometimes observed among the patrons at high-end restaurants. When we asked if anyone wanted seconds, the response was almost unanimous.

By the time the dessert course began, the guests were giddy. Sugar evokes smiles, I guess, regardless of the differences among us. Cupcakes galore, piled high with fluffy frosting and sprinkles, began making their way out of the kitchen and onto their plates.

Everyone in attendance truly seemed to love the meal and the experience, especially Nikki. All of her favorite people and all her favorite foods were in the same room with her at the same time. She was ecstatic and it showed in her contagious giggling, clapping and, most of all, her smiling eyes. Obviously, it was enough to melt all of our hearts. As the experience was coming to a close, we handed each guest a rose and a chocolate heart.

Reflecting on that incredible day, I realize just how amazing the experience was on so many levels. Nikki, against so many odds, had become a very happy twenty-one-year-old. It was a testament to how our families had blended together to support one other for the love of Nikki. We were also blessed with the unconditional love and appreciation that we received from all of the students and staff. Seeing Nikki loved, respected and appreciated as an individual by her teachers and peers, was a gift to be treasured. All of this took place on one beautiful rich day at Restaurante Dominique. We are truly a blessed family!

I met many amazing teachers, aides and administrators who had chosen to work with special needs students. They are remarkable human beings and love the kids unconditionally. Many of these people became our close friends. How can you not love people who love your children and choose to spend their days with them? These wonderful people we have met in our community have definitely been one of the silver linings that come from living in our unique world.

✦ ✦ ✦

Who Knew Because of You

If the birth of a special child is good, no one said such.
Who knew, because of you so many lives would be touched.

That winter's day before you were born
A typically joyful event made us forlorn.
In an ultrasound image we first saw you.
Heart failure or infection, it wasn't good.
They knew there were problems
and more tests were ordered.
Surely modern medicine we thought could get it sorted.

Tests revealed heart tubers and a condition called T. S. C.
The university doctors told us you just weren't meant to be.
"Her life won't be normal and she won't live past five,
That's if she makes it through term and delivery alive.
The noblest thing you can hope is she dies before birth."
God's plans differed from what they knew here on Earth.

Missed holidays and special events in the emergency room,
God's angels-on-earth helped us through the resulting doom.
Despite all our knowledge, pondering, whys, and what-ifs
Unanswered prayers are some of God's greatest gifts.

Your brother learned that different and special are OK,
And taught his schoolmates such by introducing you one day.
Your mom and brother didn't want you in
your wheelchair parked,
So with Doug, Lynley, and Nichole, against all odds,
they founded SHARP.
Severely Handicapped After-School Recreation Program,
or SHARP as it is known ,
With Wendy and Audra into Easter Seals,
SHARP and Teen-SHARP has grown.

Learning to use a spoon instead of
getting your fingers all messy,
While still enjoying events like Senior Prom
that are formally dressy.
Here you are into the young woman you have become,
Knowing your teasing and sense of humor is really quite fun.
One such as you who brings as much joy
to others is hard to find;
You have a special light, a smile, a look,
and your hugs that are so kind.
If the birth of a special child is good, no one said such.
Who knew, because of you so many lives would be touched?

Happy Birthday Nikki!!!
Love, Dad

✦ ✦ ✦

Brian was adamant that Nikki be at his college graduation in Colorado, so we decided to take a road trip. Wendy graciously offered to come with us so she could help with Nikki. She wanted us to be able to enjoy the festivities before and after graduation, and to help Brian pack for his journey back home for the summer. My mom flew out to meet us, and Steve's parents drove through the night to surprise Brian. All of the three-day-celebrations were fun and everything went off without a hitch. A great time was had by all and Nikki was on her best behavior, despite her bizarre sleep patterns.

The day we were leaving to return home happened to be Steve's fiftieth birthday. We had a little breakfast party for him with family and friends before we began the drive. Our plan was to spend the night in Las Vegas–an opportune halfway point. Brian, Steve, and I would go out for the evening to celebrate, while Wendy and Nikki could entertain themselves in the sprawling casino hotel. Wendy had never been to a casino before, so this would be a real adventure for both of them.

Once we were settled at the hotel, we took Nikki and Wendy for a tour of the casino compound. There were four floors of shops and restaurants for them to explore. It was a virtual playground, full of stimulation for Nikki. Once they felt comfortable, we were off. Wendy told us to have fun, celebrate, and not to worry about the time. She and Nikki would have fun and they would be just fine.

Following a comedy show, we had a late-night dinner and then enjoyed some casino time. We were able to relax and enjoy ourselves knowing Nikki was happy and in good hands. At 2:30 a.m., we decided to head back to the hotel. As we quietly entered the room, trying not to wake anyone, we found Nikki sitting up in her bed in total darkness clapping her hands. Uh-oh! And Wendy was also awake. She said that Nikki had fallen asleep at 10 p.m., but now it seemed like she was ready to play. We all saw this as a bad sign in terms of our own ability to sleep through the night. Bless Wendy's heart. She knew how tired we were, and that we had a full day's drive ahead of us. She decided to take Nikki for a walk around the casino so we could sleep. We gratefully collapsed on our beds, and immediately the guys' snoring symphony began. Wendy's first task was to dress both Nikki and herself in the dark. As I drifted off to sleep, I could hear Nikki's muffled giggling and Wendy rifling blindly through the suitcases. Soon, off they went, Nikki smiling from ear to ear. There was plenty for her to see and do, and she was excited to get started.

As the wee hours of the morning arrived in the casino, most of the customers had left as the cleaning crews took over. Each time Wendy took Nikki to the restroom, a security guard would follow close behind, probably because the guards weren't quite sure what or whom they were watching. Wendy just thought it was funny, and it made her feel extra safe. She and Nikki seemed to have their own security team in a city that needed it desperately. What could be better? When Nikki got tired of walking, they would find a comfortable seat in one of many closed bar lounges and hang out for a while, watching people. They kept this going until it was late enough that one of the restaurants finally opened for breakfast, and they could sit down to eat.

Afterward, we all met at the pool for a morning dip before getting on the road. That was when Wendy filled us in on the previous night's adventures. We laughed so hard that our cheeks hurt picturing the scenarios as she laid them out. It was the consensus that only Nikki could have been the central figure in such a hilarious scenario. Wendy told us that the whole time they were walking and checking out the bars, Nikki was doing her happy-hop, giving a whole new meaning to the term "barhopping." It was a sure sign she was having a good time.

Wendy told us that the experience had taken the art of people-watching to a whole new level for her. She said "considering it was my first time in Las Vegas, my eyes must have been the size of saucers staring at all those neon signs and neon people. The irony was that they were as wide-eyed about me and happy-hopping Nikki. You have to wonder, who were the real unique ones?"

"It's all a matter of where you're coming from, isn't it?"

❖ ❖ ❖

In the more normal setting of home, there were some nights that Nikki would just get out of bed, turn on her light, and play with her toys. Those were the good nights, when I could just listen for her with one ear. There were far more two-eared nights, when I had to listen carefully for problems with her seizure related breathing patterns, her head-banging, and her habit of stripping off her PJs and diaper. You get the picture. This was a classic one-ear night. I could hear Nikki awake and giggling in the next room. As that wasn't a reason to get out of bed to check on her, I stayed tucked in and floated in and out of my own dream world. As I faded a little deeper into dreamland, I saw an image of Nikki sitting on her bed, holding her toy phone up to her ear. She was smiling and having a very gleeful conversation with someone. Who could it be? I saw myself picking up the phone and putting it to my ear.

"Hello?" I asked tentatively.

From the other end came the wonderfully recognizable voice of my dad, who had passed away.

"Jeanie, is that you?" he asked.

"Yes, Dad, it's me!"

"Oh, for heaven s sake!" he belted out in a happy and hearty voice. Nikki and I have been having the BEST conversation. She is a character, you know."

"That I know." I paused, grasping for words. "Dad?"

"Yes, honey."

"Are you…okay where you are?"

"Aside from missing my dear ones, yes. I'm very happy. Not that I couldn't use some of your mom's awesome cooking, though."

I laughed, wanting our talk to go on and on. Then I became aware of clicking noises that were getting louder and louder. I thought maybe the phone line was cutting in and out, but as the wonderful dream came to a close, I realized the noise was the sound of Nikki flicking the light switch on and off in her bedroom. This has always been her direct means of communicating that she is awake, bored, and wanting some mommy-time.

Normally, I would just change Nikki's diaper, tuck her in again, kiss her good-night, and go back to bed for a few more precious minutes of sleep.

Tonight wasn't a normal night. It was a very special one. I climbed into bed with her and we assumed our favorite pretzel position.

As I lay there with her, I reflected on my dream. I will always treasure that moment as a heaven-sent gift from my dad. It reminded me that Nikki has a special gift to offer all of us, if we just take the time to listen closely.

JOURNEY TO THE MARIPOSA HOME

We had to consider Nikki's future as an adult. We began looking into options, as we knew she would eventually be leaving the nest. Where to? When? How? Would I be able to handle it when she was gone? On the flip side, would I be able to handle it if she stayed? These were some of the hardest questions I had ever had to face.

Once again, the solution appeared like a miracle. When I brought up the subject with Wendy, she told me that when her two daughters moved out in a couple of years, she wanted to open a group home for Nikki and her closest friends. Wendy felt that this was her calling in life.

"Are you serious?" I asked her.

"Yes," she said. She had already discussed it with her husband, Darren, and he was strongly considering the idea.

I knew in my heart that this would be the perfect situation for Nikki. From that moment on, I couldn't accept anything less for her. I spoke to the families of her two best friends with whom she had practically grown up. It didn't take any convincing for their parents to jump on board. We all felt it would be a win-win for everyone. However, we knew that getting a group home up and running was not going to be an easy task. It was difficult enough to get the state to approve an increase in the size of Nikki's diapers. Now we were going to have to change their policies regarding group homes.

The first thing we did was get our original SHARP committee back together, as it consisted of most of the same players. We knew exactly what we wanted, but we had absolutely no idea how to make it happen. Knowing we would have to begin the process with baby steps, we decided to meet once a week. We knew we would either have to start our own non-profit or find a way to work under an existing nonprofit's umbrella. After selecting a few local, appropriate nonprofits, we put together a proposal explaining our idea. With fingers crossed, we submitted it to one of these agencies and, weeks later, we got a positive reply. They agreed to work with us toward our lofty goal.

We looked into various models for alternative family living homes that had already been successful in other states. Then we compared and contrasted them until we found the type that we all felt was most viable. This was an incredibly long process but, by the time we were done, we knew it had all been worthwhile. Week after week, we inched our way toward our goal. Then one day, about a year-and-a-half into it, our local sponsoring agency abruptly pulled the rug out from under us. Without even offering an explanation, they said they had decided not to continue working with us on our project.

After shock, frustration, and then anger ran its course, we started over. We began talking with the managers of our regional center and held numerous meetings on the project. There were lots of promises, but no action. So we then sent a proposal to a local facility for disabled adults asking if they would be interested in setting up an off-campus, satellite group home. They liked the idea but informed us that, due to budget cuts, the state had put a freeze on funding for all new projects.

The part of our struggle that was so hard to comprehend was that the state was already in the process of changing direction. They were planning to shift more funding toward smaller group home facilities for adults with disabilities, rather than continue to fund larger facilities that were classified as institutions. This was exactly the kind of facility we were we trying to set up, but I guess we were just a little ahead of them. It took another year-and-a-half to convince the powers that be that we were all working in the same direction. Finally, after being bounced around by the bureaucratic system, we were eventually positioned to open a supported living services home project. When the state spending freeze ended, the local facility with which we had been working with agreed to let us operate under their non-profit umbrella.

We did it! Our project was finally going to become a reality in a rental house that had previously been used as a group home. By this time, Wendy and Darren had finished their training and had the certifications needed to open our group home.

Doug Brown, a member of our committee, who was also the President of a local Rotary Club, convinced his organization to take on renovating our new group home as a charitable project. Over forty men and women volunteered to paint the exterior of the house and landscape the front yard...all in just one day. At the same time, each family decorated their own child's designated room. We called them their dorm rooms, since we felt the transition would be easier if we saw it as sending our kids off to college.

With the house in good order, opening day was approaching. We appropriately named it the Mariposa Home, after the Spanish word for butterfly–keeping in mind our children were moving there to spread their wings in flight. The home had been three years in the making, but now that the time had come for Nikki to move in, I was scared. This was going to be "an empty nest syndrome" like no other. I knew in my heart it was right for Nikki, and I knew that it was right for us, but that didn't make it hurt any less. I cried throughout the process of packing Nikki's clothes and hugging all her stuffed animals and dolls. I even curled up in her bed. The move seemed much harder on me than it was on her. I wondered what my new identity would be. What would my life be like? What would I do with my third eye, the one I had grown from looking after Nikki all those years? So many questions were running through my mind. What if they dressed her differently than I did at home? What if they cut her hair differently? None of these were important in the grand scheme of things, but they were overwhelming to me at that moment.

✦ ✦ ✦

From the first day, Nikki thrived at the Mariposa Home, and continues to do so now. She actually sleeps far better there with Danielle as her roommate than she ever did at home. Their bond seems to give her a strong sense of security at night. (If I had known twenty years ago that Nikki would sleep better with a roommate, I definitely would have adopted another little girl to keep her company.) Danielle now has firsthand experience with Nikki's nocturnal activities. Some nights, Nikki gets up and crawls into bed with her. Danielle recently described the situation better in sign language than anyone could manage verbally. One evening, when Nikki

and her housemates were watching the movie, *Born to Be Wild*, there was a scene in which Katie, the gorilla, was sleeping in the van with her human friend who was taking her to safety. The scene struck a familiar chord with Danielle, and she started signing, "Same as sleeping with Nikki." They all roared with laughter.

Aside from getting a good night's sleep, another benefit of the home is that Nikki is given chores to do, and she beams with pride when she accomplishes them. Each new skill she acquires gives her an excuse to show it off.

Nikki and her friends are active in our community, and they have more of a social life than I ever will. They go bowling, swimming, shopping, and out to the movies, restaurants, and even parties and dances. They have cooking lessons, do craft projects, go on library outings, and have picnics. They even get dressed up and go to Renaissance Fairs. Their favorite outing is their yearly trip to their happy place, Disneyland. The joyous combination of Mickey Mouse ears and fast rides—it doesn't get better than that!

Another happy thing for Nikki is her personal and unique version of Facebook. Before she moved into the Mariposa Home, I put together a notebook with large pictures of the faces of our family and close friends. This has become her prized possession. She looks through it every day as an ongoing link to those who love her, while being current with the latest social media trends, in her own way.

Among the most absolutely beautiful things that have developed as a result of the Mariposa Home are the precious and enduring relationships among the clients. Equally beautiful is the dedication and commitment of the staff.

Sometimes, I think that the rose-colored lenses through which Nikki and her friends view life have unique advantages. Although their lives are challenging in ways the rest of us can not fully imagine, there is a lot they can teach us about living in the moment–about enjoying the simple fact of being. Nikki is blessed to be part of Wendy and Darren Adler's group home family. She is one of their "Adler's Angels."

WHERE WE ARE TODAY

Mom, dad, son, and daughter: we are a family. We have not lived entirely in the world of the disabled, nor have we lived entirely in the world of the abled. We have found and embraced our own middle ground. Multiple times her doctors told us Nikki was about to die and every time she proved them wrong. She is now twenty-seven years old and has taught us to never, ever let anyone take away hope, to never give up, and to never take no for an answer. Even though, at times, the challenges and sacrifices have been enormous, we look back with no regrets.

Today, Brian is in medical school, well on his way to becoming a very compassionate doctor. He has an incredible thirst for knowledge, and he wants to make a difference in the lives of others. Nikki is his catalyst. He is happily married and he and his wife, Tabetha, are soon to be parents.

As for Steve and me, we both work full time and visit Nikki at the Mariposa Home on a regular basis. We make special dates with her for outings, and she remains an integral part of all our family gatherings. Quite often, her extended family joins us for events. Nikki lets us know with unlimited hugs and kisses that she enjoys her time with us, which always makes our hearts happy. She also shows us that, when it is time, she is quite content to go back to her other home. This arrangement allows Nikki to have her own full life, while still being close to us.

There is one major bonus in this arrangement. Steve and I get a lot more sleep!

FINAL THOUGHTS

The beach has always been the place where I go to reflect. Basking in the warmth of the sun, I look toward the horizon, mesmerized by the waves. These waves, just like life, keep on coming. Some thunderous and powerful enough to knock me off my feet, and some calm, gently rolling, with the playful spray dancing on their crests. They keep on coming. That we can count on.

I watch the graceful gliding of the pelicans, breathing in sync with their relaxing rhythm. I hear the symphony of the beach grass rustle in the wind. I feel the tingling of the salt spray on my face, and I smile. The glorious expanse of the beach, with its imperfect shells glistening in the sun, has broadened everything for me now. It is where I find peace.

LOVE LETTERS TO NIKKI

My sweet Nikki,

It wasn't until your fifth birthday that I looked at myself in the mirror, and said aloud, "What the hell are you doing, ignoring Nikki, just because you're afraid you might lose her? You've already wasted the first five years of her life worrying. Well, she's still here, and she needs to know how much you love her. So stop wasting any more precious time agonizing about something over which you have no control, and just enjoy her and love her for as long as you can!"

From that moment on I have been trying to make up for lost time, expressing the affection that I have felt in my heart for you from the moment you were born. There isn't an hour of the day that I don't feel grateful that you have come into my life and blessed me and our entire family with that special kind of joy that only you are capable of giving.

Your mother, your brother, and I want you to know that you fill us with great happiness just from sharing your life with us in your own unique way. You have changed our lives in the most wonderful ways, and we could not love you more.

Your loving Dad

✦ ✦ ✦

Why Didn't They Bring Her Home?

I will never forget the devastated look on my parents' faces when they walked in and said, "Your new baby sister is sick." I was only two years old when I began my life journey with Nikki. It took me many years to realize exactly what it meant to be disabled. Yes, Nikki is that and so much more. Despite all of her challenges, she continues to enjoy life, and she teaches us every day. I learned quickly that Nikki and all other special children deserve the same respect and opportunities as so-called normal children. This idea was the driving force behind our team effort to create an after-school recreation program for them. Little did I know that the children in the program (SHARP) would end up teaching me as much, or more, than I could ever teach them. I found myself spending every spare moment enjoying their presence and watching them grow. At the same time, I was growing as an individual. Through my experiences with that program, I grew both emotionally and intellectually. I also acquired the understanding that while we all have our differences, we are all very similar inside.

After that experience with SHARP, I knew I wanted to choose a profession in which I could help others. I understood that my greatest strengths lay in working with people and assisting them in their growth and development.

Throughout my life with Nikki, I have learned so many things: patience, persistence, compassion, and the willingness to Adapt And Adjust (our family version of AAA) whenever necessary. These are life skills that will stay with me forever. The range of emotions that I have experienced with her has created my personal foundation. Nikki has allowed me to see and how to be me.

Brian, your big brother

✦ ✦ ✦

My Nikki,

Over the past twenty-seven years, I have had the good fortune to spend many joyful hours with you. Now it's time to share some of my cherished memories with you and let you know how much happiness you have brought into my life and how proud I am to call you my granddaughter.

One of my earliest recollections is of a shopping trip your aunt and I took with you when you were around three years old. In one of the stores we visited, we tried a dress on you, and the gathered skirt stuck out above your diaper. You loved it so much that you twirled around in it in front of the mirror, laughing. To complete the outfit, we found a denim hat with the brim turned up and a rose attached. You wouldn't take it off. You just kept twirling and laughing.

Another day, your aunt and I took you to the park. As soon as we arrived, you made it clear that was not where you wanted to be. So we got you back in the car and drove to the beach. But the beach didn't please you, either, and we headed back to the car. Halfway there, you plopped down on the ground. We had to inch you along slowly until we finally got you safely inside the car. Then, knowing how much you loved the hot tub, we took you directly home, got you into your swimsuit, and immersed you in the warm water. But you didn't want to be there, either. Running out of options, we rinsed you off, put you in a diaper and a big T-shirt, and sat you on your bed, near the open window, where your aunt and I sat next to you. As exhausted as we were, you were finally happy. As much as you loved the hot tub, all you wanted that day was to sit on the bed and enjoy the cool air.

You always knew how to get what you wanted. One afternoon at four o'clock we took you to get ice cream. On the next afternoon at exactly four, you grabbed my purse and keys and let me know you were ready for the same treat you had the day before. After a couple of days, your parents returned from their trip, and as soon as four o'clock rolled around, they became puzzled when you went straight for my purse and car keys.

One Christmas dinner, you leaned across the table and gave me a lingering kiss. I thought you were being your sweet self, but you were only trying to distract me long enough to scoop all the stuffing off my plate and onto your own.

I recall what an active child you were. You never sat down, and you never let me sit, either. Once when your parents were out of town, and you were staying with Boom PaPa and me, your mother called one evening. Boom PaPa answered the phone and told her that I was outside in the dark mowing the lawn with the headlights on. He chuckled that it was the only way I could find an excuse to sit down.

There was a time that Boom PaPa offered to look after you while your mommy and I went to a movie. He told us that he was planning to watch his football game on TV while we were gone. Good luck, we thought. When we came home a few hours later, he was sitting in his chair, watching the game, while holding onto your ankles and moving your legs back and forth. Your mommy and I were amazed at how happy you both seemed, and we were even a little jealous. He told us that when it was time to feed you, he took down the shower curtain from the bathroom, spread it across the floor, and sat you in the middle of it to enjoy your meal. As soon as you were finished eating, he whisked you off the curtain, scooped it up, shook it off, and hung it back in the bathroom. With minimal effort, everything was once again good to go. Clever man, Boom PaPa. He had managed to watch the entire game, and, at the same time, you were being entertained. How perfect was that?

Another time, when I knew you were coming for a visit, I wanted to do something extra special for you. I knew you liked to swing, so Boom PaPa and I bought a lawn swing and hauled it home in the back of the Cadillac, with half of it hanging out the rear. As soon as we got it home, we put it together in time for your arrival. The moment you came through the door, I took you outside to test it out. The surprise was on us, since you seemed totally disinterested. Your cousin, who was also visiting, took you out to the orchard, *instead, and pulled you around by the legs. Now, that, you loved!*

Also, knowing how much you love textures, one day, instead of water, we poured birdseed into the little swimming pool in our backyard. You sat in there happily flicking the birdseed. The next summer, thanks to your efforts, the pool was surrounded by a thick fresh growth of unusual plants.

Whenever you visited with us, Boom PaPa would sleep in the extra bedroom, and I would share the king-size bed with you. I remember your getting up at three in the morning and standing in front of the mirror, laughing. Then you would manage to open the door, and disappear down the hall. I would chase after you. This was a nightly ritual, and it always left me tired the next day. Inspired by all this nighttime activity, Boom PaPa gave you the nickname, Nik at Night, after the late-night TV show.

Life with you, dear Nikki. is a never-ending series of amazing adventures. As always, I'm looking forward to the next one.

Your loving MaMa (Grandma Helen Henderson)

✦ ✦ ✦

My dearest angel, DOMINIQUE – "Child of God"
NIKKI – "God's Angel Messenger"

Two nights before Christmas, two months before Nikki's
second birthday...
    There was Nikki, looking beautiful in her little white dress, connecting with her brother, Brian, watching and reacting to his playful antics as we celebrated the Christmas season at her great-grandmother's (Baba) house. Our spirits soared with joyful hope, observing how alert she was.

Christmas Eve Day at our annual Palace Hotel
Christmas luncheon...
    Nikki had fallen into lethargy due to a series of seizures. Little did we know that this time the toll would be a yearlong loss of the alertness we had glimpsed the evening before. An incredible sense of sadness and grief lay under my Christmas smiles that year.

Easter Sunday that same year...
    Steve and Jeanie, as always, with their amazing courage and optimism, prepared an Easter egg hunt after church for darling Brian and Nikki. Brian also had a basket to fill for his little sister, and he kept showing it to her in his loving way. As I stood in the garden holding Nikki, who looked so adorable all dressed up for Easter, all I could fearfully anticipate was another round of seizures and more near-death experiences as she fought for life. It was hard to understand how her parents were able to pick themselves up out of their own anguish each time to give such an upbeat example to us, her grandparents.
    Then, as I looked Nikki in the eyes, an incredible peace came over me. I became filled with the realization that I held an angel in my arms...that this very day was the reality, not the future. I looked around at the garden, the flowers. I felt the soft air of Pacific Grove and the sun shining down. I listened to her parents giggling

at Brian's squeals of delight with each new egg discovery. I was struck anew by the beautiful gifts God gives us.

Okay, Nikki, I remember thinking. I got your message: To live with negative "what if" only ruins the joy we have in the moment and obscures the gifts around us.

Messenger Angel

Our little Messenger Angel has given me the gift of a lifetime. I have experienced an indescribable abundance of joy and laughter with Nikki and her Family of Angels throughout the years, and I continue to do so.

Thank you, my sweet Angel, Nikki.
"Gigi" (Grandma Donna Gould)

✦ ✦ ✦

Dear Nikki,

I've known you since you were just a year old. My job as school psychologist and special education coordinator kept me in touch with your family while you were growing up. Your mother was determined to find programs that would allow you to learn and grow to the best of your ability. She refused to accept limits for you. She expected miracles and she got them. If there wasn't a program, she suggested that one should be created. She involved other parents with disabled children and inspired me to look for answers to the many difficulties they faced. You and others in your class had siblings in the schools you attended, and that helped make you an integral part of the student body.

Throughout all of the program and service development, you were the motivation for me to produce and create more services for children with multiple disabilities than I otherwise might have done. You inspired me. You were my muse. We created programs that did not exist anywhere else. I must thank you with all my heart for inspiring me to become more than I could have imagined. You are one of a kind.

Your family's motto: "We don't do normal," is both true and uplifting. None of you settled for normal; you always went for the miraculous. I love you and your family, and I will always be grateful for all you have given me and taught me.

Doug Brown,
School Psychologist, Special Education Coordinator

✦ ✦ ✦

Dear Nikki,

I learned so much as a Behavior Analyst from working with you. It has assisted me in helping other learners around the world. Here is the most important lesson you taught me: Don't ever decide that a student with multiple disabilities is incapable of learning new skills. If you do, you will miss out on such wonderful experiences and lots of love!

It was a delight every day to see how much you enjoyed pleasing the instructional staff. I fondly recall the excitement that you expressed every time you were being taught by your teacher or aides. I am a much better person and Behavior Analyst because of you and your family who have been so supportive of you, and the instructional staff who have served you.

Vicci Tucci,
Behavior Specialist

✦ ✦ ✦

Dear Nikki,

It has been over twenty years since I met you and your family. You were only five years old, but I remember how you greeted me with excitement and a big smile. You and your mother were working at a small table in the kitchen that she had set up for you to do your work. Your mom showed me what you were doing: it was a puzzle or a form board, I think. Every time you put a piece in, you got to push a dispenser to get an M&M, so you were very motivated to do your best!

Shortly after that, your mom visited my classroom. I think she liked what she saw, because soon afterwards, you were enrolled in my class, and you stayed with me for three years.

You were always a happy little girl, always excited to be in school, and to see your teachers and friends. You began participating in more and more activities, following directions given in sign language, and even signing on your own. I think some of your first signs were cracker, milk, and popsicle.

Things did not always go smoothly, though. I learned so much about teaching from you. One day you were getting angry and crying for no reason I could figure out. I asked Vicci to come watch you and me, to see if we could figure out the cause. We also talked with your mom. In the end, it was your mom who figured out what was happening. You were changing seizure drugs, and it must not have been a comfortable transition. Ever since then, I have been extra sensitive with any student making a seizure drug transition. When it was time for you to leave preschool, your mom went to Doug Brown, the Special Education Coordinator for your home district. When a classroom opened there, they chose me to be the teacher! I adored the new classroom and getting more time to work with you. That move made a huge impact on my life and my career. It is one of my happiest memories of teaching.

So you see, Nikki, when I think of you, I think of a little girl, now a young lady, who has had a long-lasting and positive influence on my life and on the lives of many other people. You gave us all an opportunity to live our dreams, to create beautiful things, and to contribute to our communities and the lives of many disabled students and their families. You taught me to be a better teacher and you helped me to see that I had the power to make positive changes for my students outside the classroom. You are truly a special angel, and I will continue to cherish your influence on my life.

**Debbie Thomas,
Teacher**

✦ ✦ ✦

Dear Nikki,

You were a magnanimous, great soul at the age of three. Your oversized spirit has guided you well into your young adult life.

Knowing you took me from teacher to learner; and, because of you, the curricula and environments you traveled in were approached in an individualized manner that motivated, educated, and, hopefully, inspired you. Horseback rider, gardener, swimmer, community helper, and shopper–these were a few of the roles I noticed you embraced.

Though you were not able to communicate with spoken words, those sparkling brown eyes proved to be full of language, and they showed everyone around you what you were observing and thinking. Your family's focus and advocacy still simmers in my heart. You have quite a fan club, Nikki. It has been a pleasure to know you and see you grow up into the lovely person you are today, one who embraces all that life brings.

My best always to you and your family and friends,

**Miss Jeanette Daniels,
Principal/Administrator**

✦ ✦ ✦

Dear Nikki,

I'll never forget the day I met you. It was my first day at the Monterey Transition Program. You walked straight up to me. The teacher signed to you to shake my hand. So, of course, you shook my hand. I just smiled and said hello. Although you couldn't hear me, you smiled back. Call me crazy, but at that moment I knew you were always going to have a special place in my heart. Seven years later, you very definitely planted yourself firmly in there.

It took three months for you to finally listen to me and trust me. Those three months were long days walking up and down the street. The first time I took you for a walk, you plopped right down not one block from the school. I had no idea what to do. You made yourself comfortable and closed your eyes so that you couldn't hear me. You were a smart girl, much smarter than people credited you with being, and I definitely caught on to that quickly. So, every day we walked, and every day you would make it a block further before you plopped down because you knew I was always going to make you walk, regardless of how long it took. It usually took the entire day! You would sit and close your eyes, and I'd just stand there and wait until you got up on your own; and we'd walk some more!

You were definitely smart enough to realize I wasn't going to let you win. Those were absolutely the most important three months with you, because we bonded. The more signs I learned, the easier it was to communicate with you and the easier it was to make you happy and make you laugh. That laugh was what I loved to hear!

Eventually, I was asked to work with you in the evenings and on weekends, and of course, I jumped right on that. Our bond turned from teacher-student to big sister-little sister although you were bigger than me, so I always call you my big little sister.

Nikki, you have definitely impacted my life greatly. You touched my heart from the moment I met you. To have had the opportunity to meet you was truly a blessing. You made me more humble and more compassionate in all aspects of my life, and you taught me the true value of not taking anything for granted, that even the impossible is possible. Just seeing your smiling face brightens my day.

You are one amazing, strong woman, and I am so grateful to be able to call you family.

Val Velasquez,
Transition Program

✦ ✦ ✦

Dear Nikki,

You are a very special person in my life. Beyond my own family, you are the most important person to me. You and I communicate in an almost spiritual way. We have a heart and mind connection that is hard to explain. I know what you need and how you feel. This helps me with you and with others who have special needs.

God gave me this gift when I was very young and I use it and listen to it every day. I believe you are one of the greatest gifts that God has given to me, and I treasure our relationship.

My life would be very empty without you in it. You are the greatest example of God's unconditional love, and I am very blessed to be surrounded by it every day.

Wendy Adler,
Your other mom at the Mariposa Home

✦ ✦ ✦

Dear Nikki,

During the many years that I have known you, I have learned some wonderful things just by being around you and caring for you. Probably the most important lesson is that of finding enjoyment in simple things, like sunshine and happy faces. You don't need any of the technology, grand distractions, or complex entertainment of this modern era. You just need a place to sit in the sun with the binder that your mother made you, filled with the faces of those you love the most. It is not in your nature, nor does it need to be, for you to desire more than that. This lesson is much like the lesson I once learned from some simple folk in the rural backcountry. Sometimes, you just need to slow down, sit in a comfortable spot, and enjoy the world around you.

Another lesson you have for all of us is how much can be said when you can't say anything at all. You communicate with actions and expressions. If you want food, you walk to the kitchen and grab a placemat, which is then set at your place at the table. You have also been known to grab my hand and place it on your chin when you need attention or comfort.

Of course, everyone can bear witness to how easily you could push through a crowd of linebackers if you decided you wanted to move past them. But those are the bold statements you make. Sometimes, you speak to us in ways both subtle and small. The look in your eyes, the smile, your clapping, and even how you rock your head at times to communicate, however subtly, just how you are feeling about the world around you.

If I had to pick a single lesson we could all learn from you, it would be your ability to love unconditionally. You may become agitated and aggressive, but this is never because of anger or hatred toward other people; it's just annoyance and frustration with the current situation. When you aren't annoyed, which is most of the time, you show great love toward those around you.

The way you light up as you approach your family and close friends is a delight to see. You express, in your unique way, a deep and abiding love that is rare and beautiful. This is mostly through your kisses, your smiles, and the way you look directly into people's eyes. Your kisses are particularly amusing and adorable, as you lean in with your lips apart and push them out as far as you can. This is your way of showing unconditional love to all of the people around you, something we all should learn to do.

Taylor Hubber,
Staff, The Mariposa Home

ACKNOWLEDGEMENTS

There are more people to thank than there are shells on the beach. Raising Nikki has truly been, and continues to be a team effort.

First and foremost, I want to acknowledge how blessed Steve and I have been to have such supportive families. We could not have managed without them. They were there for us, always ready to throw out a lifeline to help us stay afloat.

Thank you to our good friends, who supported us and listened whenever we needed to vent. They are the ones, especially my friend Melissa Feyedelem, who first convinced me to share our story.

And then there is Wendy, our other angel. God bless her and her family. I will never be able to thank them enough for everything they have done for us. I cannot even imagine what our lives would have been like without them. That's a road I wouldn't have wanted to travel. Wendy has been a daily lifeline for me since Nikki was twelve years old. Today, she is her second mom. We are extremely lucky that Nikki resides at the Mariposa Home with the rest of Adler's Angels.

So many people touched our lives throughout Nikki's school years. There are too many to name. I hope they all know how much I appreciate them. I truly believe that each and every person who chooses to work in the special education field has a halo of their own. I would especially like to thank Doug Brown. He began working with us when Nikki was only a year old, and he continues to be our friend to this day. He was the driving force behind the growth of the special-education classrooms in Pacific Grove and instrumental in making the SHARP program happen. He also played an integral part in getting the Mariposa Home up and running.

Each of you who helped us with Nikki, in our home and as her companion, will always be in our hearts, and we will always consider you part of our family.

I also want to offer a special thank you to Illia Thompson, my writing teacher, tireless cheerleader, and friend. She believed in my story and me more than I did at times. She taught me, encouraged me, and supported me. Thanks, also, to my writing classmates, who listened to my stories every week—sometimes laughing, and sometimes crying along with me.

With all these stories written, I wondered, what could I do to turn them into a book? That was the point when Kathleen Sonntag and Roberta Edgar came into my life and agreed to be my editors. For them to make this book happen, they had to dive headfirst into our life's crazy journey. They, along with the guidence and encouragement from Amy Taylor and Victoria Foster from Reel Books, worked endless hours helping me turn my dream of writing this book into a reality. Without their tireless efforts and those of Owen Sonntag and the many amazing friends who offered to proofread (LindaWinchester, Margie McLaughlin, Flo Allen, Barbara Mooder, Illia and Doug), you would not be holding this book today.

Now with the manuscript proofread and ready to go, what do I do next? This took a village of friends, and friends of friends, many who don't want credit for all their hard work (but they know who they are). To all these individuals, I shall be forever grateful.

Last, but certainly not least, I want to thank Steve, Brian and his wife, Tabetha, for their continued love and support.

21940561R00116

Made in the USA
San Bernardino, CA
12 June 2015